THE

Crystal Witch

THE MAGICKAL WAY TO CALM AND HEAL
THE BODY, MIND, AND SPIRIT

**SHAWN
ROBBINS**

**LEANNA
GREENAWAY**

STERLING ETHOS
New York

STERLING ETHOS
New York

An Imprint of Sterling Publishing Co., Inc.
1166 Avenue of the Americas
New York, NY 10036

This publication is intended for informational purposes only. This publication includes alternative therapies
that have not been scientifically tested. The publisher does not claim that this publication shall provide
or guarantee any benefits, healing, cure, or any results in any respect. This publication is not intended to
provide or replace conventional medical advice, treatment, or diagnosis or be a substitute to consulting with
a physician or other licensed medical or healthcare providers. The publisher shall not be liable or
responsible in any respect for any use or application of any content contained in this publication or any
adverse effects, consequence, loss, or damage of any type resulting or arising from, directly or indirectly, the
use or application of any content contained in this publication. Any trademarks are the property of their
respective owners, are used for editorial purposes only, and the publisher makes no claim of ownership and
shall acquire no right, title, or interest in such trademarks by virtue of this publication.

ISBN 978-1-4549-3468-4

Distributed in Canada by Sterling Publishing Co., Inc.
^{c}/o Canadian Manda Group, 664 Annette Street
Toronto, Ontario, Canada M6S 2C8
Distributed in the United Kingdom by GMC Distribution Services
Castle Place, 166 High Street, Lewes, East Sussex, England BN7 1XU
Distributed in Australia by NewSouth Books,
University of New South Wales, Sydney, NSW 2052, Australia

For information about custom editions, special sales, and premium and corporate purchases, please contact
Sterling Special Sales at 800-805-5489 or specialsales@sterlingpublishing.com.

Manufactured in China

4 6 8 10 9 7 5

www.sterlingpublishing.com

Interior design by Sharon Jacobs
Cover design by Elizabeth Mihaltse Lindy
Picture credits – see page 298

To the Past, the Present,
and the Future.

—SHAWN ROBBINS

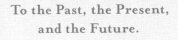

With affection and gratitude,
I dedicate this book to my stepfather,
John Greenaway.
Your care and support has
meant so much to me
over the years.

—LEANNA GREENAWAY

Contents

Part One

LEARN CRYSTAL WITCHCRAFT

Part Two

EXPLORE
MORE CRYSTAL MAGICK

Shawn Robbins

One rainy Monday, I was scouring eBay for some old copies
of *Prediction* magazine. I finally found what I was looking for:
someone was selling a whole heap of them, so I nonchalantly
placed a bid. To my delight, I won the auction and a few days
later, a very large stash of used magazines showed up at
my apartment. I unpacked the parcel, and there on the top
was an old copy of *Fate and Fortune*. I went to set it aside,
but it fell to the floor and opened at Leanna's column.
I was powerfully drawn to it. As I started to read, I knew
immediately that we were connected and that somehow,
we had to write a book together. My psychic senses
screamed at me to email Leanna and present the idea.
This is how we met, and, four books later, we
are still united in our writing.

Deanna Greenaway

I was shocked, to say the least, when I received Shawn's email. I had always slaved over my column and written books on my own, so venturing into a joint project seemed a little strange to me at first.

Having said all that, something enigmatic happens when Shawn and I write together. She is in the US and I am in the UK, yet somehow, across these many thousands of miles, we are synced to perfection. It's like we are sisters, operating from different parts of the world, having the same thought process along the way.

One night, after sleeping terribly, I woke up abruptly at around 6:00 a.m. I heard the words "crystal craft" being whispered into my ear, and I knew it was a spirit voice giving me an idea for our next book. Shawn said that we were once again being guided. With a smiling heart, we offer you our book on crystal witchery. We hope you enjoy!

The Basics of Wicca and Crystals

CRYSTALS ARE USED AND TREASURED BY ALMOST EVERY culture, religion, and society. For centuries, royals all over the world have donned priceless studded crowns that have been coveted. Crystals have been incorporated into glamorous jewelry and used as healing or magickal talismans. They have been celebrated, fought over, and displayed with pride. We mine crystals, revere them for their beauty, and even use them in modern technology. They contain the planet's DNA, stamped with millions of years of evolutionary history.

Why is it that even today, we regard these cherished gemstones with such intensity, and why is it that we carry on these time-honored fascinations? It is probably because crystals embody magick. These captivating, enchanting stones carry so much mysticism that even today, we can't fully understand the extent of their power.

CRYSTALS: A BRIEF OVERVIEW

By the time a crystal lands in the palm of your hand, it has likely lived a very storied existence. Maybe the stone you hold was passed down from generation to generation. Perhaps it was buried deep within the walls of a cave, inside a volcano, or in a hydrothermal spring. It may be hundreds or thousands or even millions of years old. Some diamonds were formed more than 3 billion years ago!

A quick internet search or browsing of your local library's shelves will reveal countless sources of information regarding crystals, stones, and minerals and how each variety is connected to a long and sometimes complicated history. One thing that has remained consistent since ancient times is our interest in gemstones and their inherent power. And, as you'll learn throughout this book, crystals are every bit as relevant, useful, and valued today as they were thousands of years ago.

When we talk about crystals, it is important to make some distinctions, especially since they are sometimes confused or spoken about in the same breath with other materials. Atoms and ions are the building blocks of crystals. It's the way the atoms and ions group together and arrange themselves internally in a regular, systemic, and symmetric order—the crystal structure—that makes a substance crystalline. Crystals also must have the same amount of negative and positive charge, which makes them balanced. Minerals are naturally occurring crystalline solids.

As you read this book, you'll discover that crystals have energetic properties and healing qualities, and you may be inclined to purchase some for your own use. You can find almost any of them online, of course, and you may also be fortunate enough to have a New Age shop with crystals nearby. But sometimes people really want to buy local—they want to know that the stone they are working with has a history with the region and perhaps even draws some energy from it.

Semiprecious vs. Precious

Let's also clear up the nomenclature of *semiprecious* versus *precious* stones. Diamonds, rubies, sapphires, and emeralds are considered the traditional precious stones. *Semiprecious* is the category that holds everything else: any stone of lesser value than a diamond, ruby, sapphire, or emerald. Yet the term semiprecious is often misleading in terms of how rare or expensive a stone might be. A rare garnet might be many times more expensive than a low-quality diamond. Therefore, the classifications of *semiprecious* and *precious* are falling out of favor these days, especially for gemologists. For witches, all gemstones are considered precious and valuable.

A Word on Manmade Crystals

Naturally, you might ask whether a laboratory-created crystal has the same properties as one from nature. There are two schools of thought on this: Die-hard naturalists believe that only real crystals can work for healing and shifting energy, as these stones contain the stories and energies of everything they've touched. On the other hand, many healers feel that if a stone speaks to you on an energetic level, it's going to work with and for you, no matter its source.

In other words, don't worry so much about where a crystal came from, as long as you connect with it. Realistically, you will not always know the complete history of a natural crystal, which is part of its mystique. On the other hand, if you have a brand-spanking-new crystal to work with, the two of you can really sync with each other.

The benefit of manmade crystals, of course, is that they are often much less expensive than those that have been mined. If a manufactured crystal is what your budget can handle, keep in mind that you will infuse it with love and energy. It will work just fine.

ALTAR CRYSTALS
Creating a Magickal Workspace

The altar is a sacred space unique to every witch. This is where the magick happens; it's a place where you can worship your chosen deities and, above all, connect with your inner witch. The size of the altar is insignificant. You can have a large table set out somewhere in your home, or you can use the top of a sideboard. Some witches prefer to use a small coffee table or the kitchen worktop. There is also no need to have it on view all the time. You might opt for a portable altar and keep all your belongings in a chest under the bed. Lots of witches shy away from broadcasting their Wiccan faith, but really Wicca is becoming more and more popular.

The items on your altar must appeal to you. If you worship angelic vibrations, you might like an angel ornament or a picture of an angel somewhere on the surface. If you favor the Mother Goddess's energy, you may want to put something on your altar that represents her. (If you own a copy of our book *The Witch's Way*, you can find a list of angels and goddesses that influence particular situations, alongside the types of crystals, herbs, and other items that work best with your chosen spells.)

This is *your* altar, so you can decide what to place on it, but there are a few essential items that every witch should have on hand. If you are already an established practitioner of Wicca, feel free to skim through this section, as it is an overview.

Colors in Witchcraft

Witches rely heavily on color magick. Different colors can signify different intentions or themes, so certain candles and items should be specifically colored when used in spells. Before reaching into your candle drawer or laying out your altar cloth, consider which color will work best to promote your specific intention.

BLACK is often avoided in spellcasting because it is commonly used in dark magick. However, more experienced witches can use black to banish anything or anyone negative. If used correctly, it can be beneficial.

BLUE stands for truth, wisdom, stable emotions, meditation, psychic insight, protection, and patience.

BROWN can help you tune in to the natural world. It assists with concentration and decision-making and can be used in matters related to friendship, including relationships with animals.

GOLD is the color used for monetary matters, triumph in competition, improving intelligence, promoting health, and rejuvenation of the mind, body, and spirit.

GREEN bolsters spells for money, prosperity, success, and luck. It is helpful with career matters and with fertility.

ORANGE helps with business matters (including selling property), memory, and stamina. If you need to find lost property, decrease your fears, favorably settle legal issues, or succeed in a new job, then work some orange into your altar.

PINK works well for compassion and spiritual healing, and in mending broken relationships. You can also rely on pink to improve existing relationships or to attract love.

PURPLE promotes peace, healing, spiritual protection, and psychic visions. It can be helpful for those wishing to practice astral projection. For everyday, practical rituals, use purple to boost business, help in the search for a new job, and influence anything to do with investments.

RED helps with intentions focused on courage, passion, and strength. The energy of red can increase one's attractiveness and keep enemies at bay.

SILVER boosts psychic abilities (including intuition), decreases the negative energy of the mind or environment, clarifies dream visions, and helps one connect with the Mother Goddess.

WHITE calls on angels and spirit guides, invokes those who have passed, encourages harmony in relationships or environments, and purifies a home. White can also be viewed as the blank canvas of colors; it can be used in any ritual.

YELLOW helps with creativity, learning, and concentration. It increases energy and provides protection while one is traveling. This color also helps with matters concerning the head, including headaches and mood swings.

Altar Cloth

Consider your altar cloth colors when performing spells (refer to Colors in Witchcraft on pages 6–7). For example, if you are conducting a healing spell, you would use yellow or gold candles, so in this instance, you'd opt for a yellow or golden cloth. For love, the color is primarily pink, so a cloth in a shade of pink would be used to represent romantic or family situations. If you're not sure, a white or purple cloth is probably the safest bet. These will give your workspace the right energy to begin. Purple is the principle spiritual color and imparts a powerful angelic vibe, whereas white is neutral and symbolizes purity. Nature-based witches have been known not to use any cloth at all; they prefer to set out their altar on natural wood. These are guidelines. The choice is yours.

Candles

Placed near the back of the altar, you should have two large tapered or chub-like candles, one to the left and the other to the right. These two candles should be white, because it's a neutral color representing purity. Before a spell begins, light the candles. Blow them out to reuse again once the spell is complete. You can also incorporate tea lights, selecting colors based on your spell's intention.

Pentacle

The pentacle (also known as a pentagram) is the heart of the altar and should sit directly in the center of the ritual space. Each point of the star represents one of the five elements: earth, air, fire, water, and spirit.

You can make your own pentacle or purchase one. The size is unimportant; you can use a small pentagram charm or draw one on a piece of paper. It's just the representation that you are looking for. Always have your pentacle facing you in the upright position so that it resembles a human (center point at the top, two side points symbolizing the arms, and the lower points indicating the legs).

The Elements

Although the pentagram represents the five elements—earth, air, fire, water, and spirit —you also need symbolic representations on your altar. The only element you cannot represent physically is the spirit; you will instead call upon that when you begin to cast your spells. Re-create the other four elements by placing items on the altar that represent each of them. Options for each include:

EARTH   Sand, dirt, leaves, bark, flowers, twigs, salt, metals, ceramic, an image of the earth, rocks and stones, acorns and seeds

AIR   Bell, incense, a wand, a fan, a sword, feathers, wind chimes, faerie figurines or images, cloud images

FIRE   Candles, dragon figurines or images, lighters or matches, sun images, volcanic stones

WATER   Rainwater or naturally sourced water (often poured into a chalice or ceremonial goblet), driftwood, seaweed, seashells, mermaid figurines or images, mirrors, crystal balls, scrying bowl, oceanic images

INCORPORATING CRYSTALS

When it comes to spellcasting, it's important not to blend the energies of several different types of crystals at any one time. You should never have more than two different gems on the altar unless the spell calls for it. Remember that these magickal stones let off their own respective energies, and they may become conflicted. This will result in a spell that doesn't work as well as you intended. For example, if you are using amethyst as your primary crystal, it is quite all right to have multiple amethysts present on the altar—they will let off the same vibe. But think twice about putting a piece of labradorite or rose quartz next to an amethyst.

The main rule of thumb is that every item placed on your altar should have a purpose. This sacred space has a job to do, so you need to take your time and choose your items carefully.

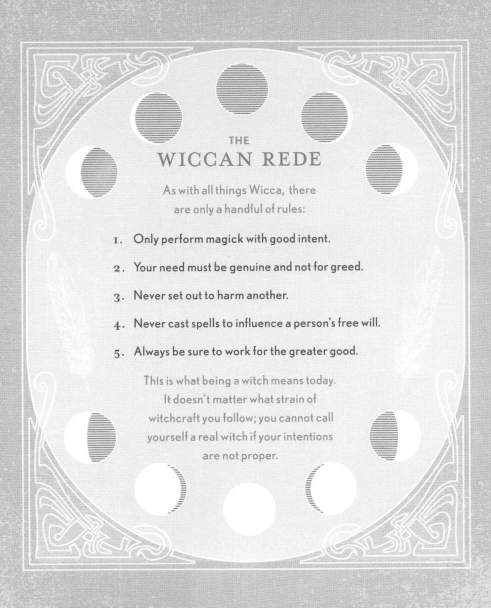

THE
WICCAN REDE

As with all things Wicca, there
are only a handful of rules:

1. Only perform magick with good intent.

2. Your need must be genuine and not for greed.

3. Never set out to harm another.

4. Never cast spells to influence a person's free will.

5. Always be sure to work for the greater good.

This is what being a witch means today.
It doesn't matter what strain of
witchcraft you follow; you cannot call
yourself a real witch if your intentions
are not proper.

Part One

LEARN CRYSTAL WITCHCRAFT

Chapter 1

What Is a Crystal Witch?

USING CRYSTALS ALONGSIDE MAGICK IS COMMON practice today, and whether you are experienced in your traditions or an inexperienced witch who has just discovered the craft, at some point in the future you will almost definitely begin to use a lot of different stones in your spell work.

If you have read some of the other books in the Modern-Day Witch series, you will know that witches fall into a variety of categories, with each sect focusing on various parts of the craft that ring true to them. Some may give more emphasis to candle magick, for instance, whereas others, like hedge witches and kitchen witches, might prefer working with potions, pouches, and herbs. The term *crystal witch* means that crystals and gemstones are the main focus of that witch's craft.

Many crystal witches belong to the eclectic witch category. Eclectic witches tend to pull on many different aspects of witchcraft to carve out their own path, which makes their faith personal and custom-tailored to them. This is the beauty of Wicca. We all go through life at our own pace, and you can interweave the parts of Wicca that give you a sense of truth.

Before you embark on your journey toward crystal craft, you need to know that becoming a crystal witch—or any type of witch—will not just happen overnight. It can take many years of study and practice to evolve into the role entirely. Many experienced crystal witches are incredibly knowledgeable and proficient when it comes to their understanding of stones, and because there are so many crystals the world over, the time it takes to reach this level of familiarity is understandable. Before writing this book, Shawn and I both felt that we had broad-enough knowledge on the subject to incorporate our findings into a manuscript, but along the way, and with a lot of research, even we learned a thing or two we didn't know before!

As a crystal witch, you might not use crystals just for spell work; you may also use them for one or more of the following:

CHAKRA BALANCING Some witches are skillful when it comes to knowing the right crystals to use when aligning your body's *chakras*, or energy centers. They might also make chakra bracelets or other forms of jewelry to help a person equalize their energies.

DIVINATION Clairvoyant witches scry using crystal balls by gazing into a faceted stone to reveal the future. They might also dowse with crystal pendulums to receive answers from the spirit world or to find energy fields, such as ley lines.

HEALING Gemstones are often used as a healing accompaniment, placed on affected parts of the body to alleviate pain or discomfort.

MEDITATION Certain crystals have the power to transform meditations, raising a person's vibration or enabling the art of astral projection.

POTIONMAKING This is the practice of infusing crystals in water to create elixirs, which are later consumed as magickal potions. Please be aware that some crystals are toxic, so your knowledge of gemstones must be very significant if this is the path you wish to take. There are also stones that rust or dissolve in water, so you must be sure to use a safe and hardy crystal for this purpose.

HOW DOES CRYSTAL MAGICK WORK?

Crystals flourish and grow within the earth's crust, sometimes taking millions of years to form and develop. As they mature and expand, they begin to oscillate and vibrate, encapsulating powerful elements from the earth, the oceans, the sun, and the moon. Although technically, crystals are not scientifically classified as living creatures, we believe that each crystal is alive with its own unique energy force.

As well as being valuable for their mystical and magickal properties, crystals are also utilized for industry. In modern technology we use fine slivers of quartz crystal to help regulate frequencies and enable correct movements for pinpoint accuracy. An example of this can be found in watches and clocks. We also use quartz in microprocessors and radios.

In the New Age spiritual movement, many cultures believe that crystals radiate high frequencies and, if placed on certain parts of the body, enable one's internal chakras to align. There is no scientific basis to show that crystals possess or project anything that affects our natural bodies, but that doesn't mean they don't! If crystals communicate with technology, such as computer chips, then surely it is possible for them to communicate in other ways. Some skeptics reject the power of stones used for healing and consider them to have nothing more than a placebo effect, but there are many people who believe wholeheartedly in the power of crystals. For now, we can only wait until science provides a verdict on their abilities.

Crystals are most commonly known for their therapeutic properties, and many healers spanning diverse cultures use them to balance a person's energy and help combat any ailments. While you can employ crystals for help with any number of ailments, please know that they are not a replacement for modern medicine and should not be relied upon to cure illnesses. Please consult with your doctor as needed.

Witches have used crystals for centuries as part of their magickal practices and believe that each one holds an inherent power that projects itself toward enhancing a person's life. These precious nuggets of power are not just earthbound; they are universal. In this book, you will come to learn exactly how to get the best out of your stones and how to tap into them to enrich your life.

CHOOSING AND COLLECTING YOUR MAGICKAL STONES

These days it is so easy to hop online and instantly find what you are looking for when it comes to selecting magickal items to use in spellcasting. You can access all kinds of paraphernalia, such as herbs, candles, and even powerful spices from all over the globe, and have them in your possession with just the click of a button. However, if your focus is entirely on crystal magick, you may have more success by venturing out to visit a store. Some people who practice crystal craft believe that we should never purchase stones without seeing them first. Their argument is that each individual stone emanates a different kind of energy—energy that might not necessarily work for your intended task. Though there is no true right or wrong way to attain crystals, it's recommended that you be selective and get a real feel for the stone you're interested in acquiring. It's like inviting a new friend into your life, a magickal companion who can assist you in all manner of witchery for an entire lifetime. Having said that, if you are housebound, don't drive, or don't live near a town with a New Age shop, it is perfectly acceptable to purchase crystals from the web or through a mail-order service. Your stone will still work. You will just need to spend more time familiarizing yourself with it once it arrives, spending as much as a week cleansing it and blending its energy with your own.

Should you choose to visit a brick-and-mortar store, then, before you step foot through the door, it is vital that you research what type of crystal you need. Make sure you are seeking out the correct stone for the task at hand. In this book, we have made this process easier for you by providing an A–Z guide for all the most commonly used crystals, along with their magickal correspondences (see chapter 4, pages 56–96). You can scroll through the lists and see at a glance which crystal might work best for your situation. Only once you have educated yourself and made your choice can you begin to seek out the right stone for the job.

Make a Crystal-Clear Connection

Once inside the store, your main goal is to make a connection with a stone. Every crystal on the planet contains fluctuating levels of power depending on when and where it was sourced. Some have more strength than others, regardless of size. You may have visited New Age shops and seen very large crystal geodes standing proudly in all their glory. These stunning creations are indeed full of superpower and would surely grace any spell, but believe it or not, smaller tumbled stones—rocks or minerals that are rounded and polished—can be just as effective when used in rituals. It is safe to say that you don't have to spend hundreds of dollars on a crystal when a smaller, more affordable one will do the trick just fine.

Many proprietors or employees of crystal shops have vast knowledge of the varieties and uses of crystals, so if you are in any doubt at all, you can always ask them to point you in the right direction. They may be able to recommend a few different types of crystals to help solve the issue at hand. However, the key to finding the right stone is to take your time. Before you even think of purchasing a crystal, you must be clear about what you are trying to achieve.

Each crystal has its own purpose, so the process of selecting the perfect stone should not be rushed. Leave yourself plenty of time to really browse the store and the selection of stones. Remember, you are choosing a companion to help you with a purpose, so don't ever be embarrassed about how long it takes for you to choose. If the salesperson is looking at you funny as you linger over many different rose quartz tumbled stones, for example, just explain that you are taking your time because you will be in it for the long haul— this will be your next crystal buddy. This selection

process is your job, and yours alone, so never be tempted to ask the assistant to help you pick the actual stone you will take home.

Another point to mention is that after entering a crystal shop, you may feel a little odd. Many people report headaches or feelings of light-headedness or nausea upon spending time in crystal shops. This is completely normal. It shows that you are sensitive to the energies around you, especially when facing many varieties of crystals all being housed in the same place. Their combined vibrations can be overpowering, so you must learn how to first tune out the other crystals before you begin to tune in to the variety you need.

When you're standing before the crystal display, attempting to make your choice, you can assist yourself by asking the universe for some guidance. Practice some deep breathing, focus on your intention (to find the perfect stone), and try a little incantation, like *"I ask for positive direction in making this connection"* or *"I ask for a crystal that will help me find focus"* (or love, or peace, or healing—whatever it is you're looking for). Your experience will be different every time you choose a crystal. This is because each stone has a personality of its very own, an aura that belongs only to it, and you must make sure that you select the one whose energy can merge with your own.

Listening for Your Crystal

Your perfect crystal might be on a shelf or inside a glass cabinet. It could be in a box alongside a lot of other, similar stones. Your eyes might be immediately drawn to it, or it may sing out to you, saying, *"Look at me," "Pick me up," "Choose me."* You must pay attention to these feelings if they arise and do as your instincts suggest. If no crystal catches your eye, try one of the following techniques to determine which stone is right for you.

Cast your eyes over the various crystals before you and, for a few minutes, concentrate on each stone. Focus on the color and cut of each one, notice any grains or imperfections, and study its symmetry. Do any of them appeal specifically to you? Is there one quality that jumps out at you?

Hover your left hand (the hand nearest the heart) over the top of the collection or one specific stone, and see if you feel any energy radiating from them/it. It's a bit like using a metal detector, only you are the sensor. Some crystals won't emit anything at all, and others might make you feel tingly, hot, or very cold, as if your hand were in a freezer. Any kind of sensation—be it hot, cold, tingly, or even throbbing—simply means you are responsive to the crystal and it will work for you in a magickal way. The fact that every crystal is different cannot be stressed enough.

You really must deliberate over your choice, because one crystal might release heat while another just next to it lets off a cooler vibration.

When you pick up the crystal that you believe speaks most clearly to you, cup it in both hands. Stay in this position for a few minutes, trying to detect any vibrations. You need to make sure you feel something. If you sense nothing at all, then it's not the crystal for you and you can put it back where you found it.

Another good way to tap into the power is to hold it up to your Third Eye Chakra. This is the space between both of your eyes. Hold it there (again, with your left hand) and close your eyes. What do you see? Do you feel a kind of rapport with the stone? You can purchase as many crystals as you like on any given trip, but it's best to select only one or two when you are feeling for the connection.

You might find that more than one crystal will catch your eye, and then you could become confused, not knowing which one to choose. If this occurs, place one stone in each of your hands and grasp them tightly, making a fist around each one. Does one of your hands begin to throb? Do you feel your pulse in your fingertips? Does one of your arms start aching or become tender or sensitive? As uncomfortable as this may be, it is exactly what you need to be feeling. This is how the crystal communicates with you, and, in doing so, projects powerful rays, amalgamating its energy with your aura.

Another great way to get a real feel for a crystal is to draw the stone slowly toward your body. Again, pay attention to how to feel. One or more of your chakras may start to react. You may experience a twinge in your solar plexus, upper chest, or forehead. This is a sure indication that your energies are aligning and that this could be the crystal for you.

Never just look at a stone and say to yourself, "Wow, that looks pretty! I'll buy it." Some of the most effective crystals are the odd, ugly-looking ones tucked away at the back of a box. They might not be as aesthetically pleasing to the eye, but they could hold a power that might just make the difference between a good spell and a great one!

Once you have settled on your choice, you're ready to get to know this beautiful stone. Many witches like to perform a ritual with each new crystal they obtain, to welcome it into the fold. You can call it a meet-and-greet, an initiation, or a crystal orientation—it's all the same.

Welcome Your Crystal Companion

Before beginning this ritual, it is important that you be in the right frame of mind. If you have had a bad day or your mood isn't sweet, leave the welcoming to another time. This ritual should be seen as a quiet time to focus, so make sure that you remove all sources of chaos.

When you feel ready, choose a space with natural light so you can easily see the interior of the crystal. Put on relaxing music and light a single white candle. Sit in a comfortable position and take the crystal in your hand.

Take some deep breaths. Close your eyes and feel the weight of the crystal in your hand. Begin with an opening incantation, calling down the universe to help you.

"I call upon the angels, gods, and goddesses to assist me this day.
Allow me to connect with my newfound stone and share in its magick."

Open your eyes. Hold the crystal where you can see it and study it. Observe its shape, its facets, its points— all its various dimensions. Focus on the interior of the crystal. What do you observe? How does the light enter and play inside the stone? You might even feel drawn to the internal structure as though in a kind of mystical trance. Remember, there is not another crystal exactly like this one, the one you have chosen as a partner.

It is not uncommon to occasionally run into a bit of a standstill during these welcoming rituals. If you find you're having trouble connecting with your crystal on an energetic plane, simply light a white candle (if you haven't done so already), hold the stone loosely, and say aloud:

"Universe, I am open to the energy around me.
Help me to forge a connection with this crystal."

Allow the candle to safely burn down (with supervision). Carry the stone around or have it nearby for the rest of the day. Touch and stroke the crystal whenever you can, even if you are simply sitting and watching TV. The more you handle it, the better. Some witches even insist on sleeping with their new stones at night for up to a month. They place them under the pillow, tuck them inside their pillowcase, or keep them on the nightstand by the bed. This is completely up to you.

You may want to repeat this welcoming process with your crystal from time to time, as a way of replenishing your connection or as a special thank-you if the crystal has been particularly useful or helpful.

Crystal Gifts

Some people believe that a crystal will find you. It is strange how this happens, and it can transpire in many ways. If on the rare occasion you ever find a crystal lying around or see one on the pavement or anywhere in passing, you must pick it up. Everything that sits in your path is part of your destiny, so the reason for a crystal's appearance will be apparent only to you. Neither author of this book has been lucky enough to find one lying around, but if we did, we would be sure to interpret it as a clear message that it was meant to be.

There are times when you won't need to seek out a crystal by leaving your home or finding it online; it will find you. For instance, friends or loved ones might give you tumbled stones or crystal jewelry as a gift. It's during these moments that we must rely on the instincts of others to choose the crystal meant for us. If you are given earrings, a bracelet, or a necklace, you can connect with the object by wearing it for at least seventy-two hours without taking it off. You might also like to place it under your pillow to sleep with for at least a week. During the night, its energy will attach to yours. It's a slower process but will work just as well in the end.

PREPARING YOUR CRYSTAL
FOR MAGICK

Lots of witches the world over include a crystal in every single spell they perform. The frequency of use is up to the individual, but using magickal stones alongside rituals is becoming more popular with each passing year.

Crystals really give spells that magickal punch, so including them in rituals is important, especially if you want to ensure success. Believe it or not, for literally every situation you might face, there are numerous gemstones that can be used. For example, if you are casting a spell for better health, you can find thirty or more stones that could potentially work for you. The more familiar you become with crystals, minerals, and stones and the more confident you are in using them, then the sooner you will learn which can serve you best. A little research beforehand is a definite must. Each stone has a slightly different magickal influence compared to the next, making it perfect for pinpointing specific issues.

ADVICE FROM LEANNA

I am quite superstitious about when I choose my crystals. Unless I stumble upon one I like and acquire it on impulse, I usually only go shopping for my stones on a new moon phase. This is purely my choice, and I suppose it really doesn't matter that much, but I love the new moon and like to introduce my newfound beauties when the energies are in this phase.

Chapter 2

Crystal Management

CARING FOR YOUR CRYSTALS

I F YOU'VE SPENT SOME TIME SEEKING AND STOCKPILING crystals, you may find that you have acquired quite a collection. With this in mind, perhaps your next question about crystal witchcraft is "How do I store my crystals?" There isn't any right or wrong method, and each witch tends to follow their instincts and do it their own way. There are, however, a few factors to consider. Crystals need care and consideration; if you want them to perform at their very best, you will need to treat them with respect.

POSITIONING AROUND THE HOME

Crystals do not just project power; they also act like sponges and absorb the energy around them. With this in mind, it's important to consider where in the home you'll store your crystals. Perhaps you might like to have your stones out on display, arranged on a shelf or a dresser. If you opt to store your stones in this way, consider that the crystal's energy could become contaminated. Visitors are often drawn to the beauty of stones and might casually pick them up. This will transfer another person's energy onto your crystals, and they will need to be cleansed before their next use.

The preferred placement and storage of a crystal can also change depending on the variety. For example, placing amethyst or citrine on a windowsill is not a good idea, as these varieties are highly pigmented and will sadly fade if exposed to sunlight.

For larger raw clusters or display pieces not used for magick, leaving them out is quite acceptable, but ritual crystals need to be kept as pure as possible. The best way to house them is in a special drawer or box. For smaller tumbled stones, I favor craft boxes with individual compartments. Unfortunately some of these can be pricey, but a more inexpensive way to get your hands on this method of storage is by making your own. You can do this by obtaining any box. A cardboard or candy box works well, especially when ice cube trays are placed inside, acting as an ideal way to keep all your stones separate. A small label positioned inside each compartment can also be helpful for reminding yourself what each stone is called and what spells it might be used for. (You can also keep such notes in your Book of Shadows.) You can then situate this storage box inside a drawer, making it easy to find what you need.

Some witches like to wrap larger crystals in red cloth. This color has the slowest rate of energy absorption, so it acts as an energy barrier. Just be sure that the fabric has natural fibers; crystals do not respond well to synthetic materials. Stick to pure cotton or wool, or maybe source a red nonsynthetic velvet drawstring pouch or bag.

If you have more than one kind of stone, try to separate them according to their variety. This way the energy of one stone won't spill into the crystal sitting next door to it.

CRYSTAL CLEANSING AND CHARGING

We have established that crystals absorb power from their surroundings. While they can attract positive energy, they can also hold on to negative energy. Also consider what you've been using the crystal for. Crystals that are used in clearing negative energy should be cleansed before being used again. You might notice that after such a ritual, your crystal will feel hot or heavy, or look particularly lackluster. You're not imagining things; the stone is just doing its job and removing unwanted energy from a chakra or aura. If you have a crystal you've been relying on for some time and it seems to have lost its *oomph*, you should think about giving it a reasonable cleanse and recharge. A regular crystal cleansing will not only recharge your gems; it will rid them of all invisible debris. Some people like to purify regularly and perform a cleansing once a month. For magickal uses, it is always best to cleanse your crystals before and after any ritual. There are multiple ways to do this, so here we have listed a few to get you started.

Smudging with Sage

Sage bundles act as a spiritual disinfectant. They can be purchased from any New Age store or online. Using a lighter or match, carefully light the end of the sage bundle in a safe area—outside or in a nonflammable area. Let it burn for a few moments, then blow out the flames. (Please exercise caution; your sage bundle should *never* be completely engulfed in flames.) With your crystal in one hand and the sage bundle in the other, waft the crystal through the smoke for about thirty seconds. You will find that this is a quick and efficient method of purification; it's one of the most common methods used by witches today.

Freshwater Bath

Submerging your stones in water from a running stream, spring, pond, or lake is a natural and effective method of cleansing. Be aware, though, that you cannot use this method with some crystals. Celenite can dissolve, and hematite will rust when left in water too long. For stones with sensitivity to liquids, the smudging technique described previously is a safer bet.

Saltwater Bath

You can cleanse many crystals with a salt water rinse or bath. Just fill a glass or ceramic bowl with salt water—a palmful of sea salt should suffice for a quart of water, and less salt for less water—and place your crystal(s) in it. You can allow it to soak for as little as one hour, but if you think your crystal has been loaded down with a particularly heavy energy, you can leave it in to soak for up to one week. When your cleanse is complete, rinse your stone in cool spring water and toss the salt bath away.

If you live near the sea, you can place your crystals near the water's edge and bathe them in the ocean water for a few minutes. If you have too many crystals to take to the beach, collect the sea water in a clean bottle and immerse the stones in the water when you're back home.

Note that some stones can be damaged by salt—generally anything that's porous (like opal) or has high water content. Pyrite, hematite, and lapis lazuli should not be soaked in salt water. For these stones, it is best to use the smudging technique.

If you're lucky enough to have a large, crystal-holding geode with a cavity, you can use it cleanse other crystals very successfully. Geodes are known for their ability to neutralize negative energy and replace it with positive vibes. Crystals should be placed inside of the geode cavity for at least twenty-four hours.

Sunlight and Moonlight

Light from the sun and the moon not only cleanses your crystals—it also can be used to give them a recharge. Placing your stones outside during the day or overnight to soak in the rays will provide them with a boost. You can lay them on the ground, on an outside table, or on a windowsill. It's recommended, no matter whether you cleanse during the day or during the night, that you do so during a full moon phase, as it's a time when magickal happenings take place.

However, if you really can't wait for the full moon to arrive, make sure that, whatever the phase, the sun or the moon is at least visible in the sky. To revitalize your crystals during the daytime, leave them outside when the sun is at its brightest. This is a quick cleanse that only takes a few hours, but again, make sure that light-sensitive crystals such as citrine and amethyst are not left in the heat of the sun for more than thirty minutes—they will fade.

Sea Salt

Pure sea salt can be purchased from any local store and is a good way to rid your crystal of imperfect vibes. Pour the salt into a large-enough bowl, making sure that the crystals are completely covered. Don't touch them for a few hours. You can also substitute earth, clay, or sand for salt. Always dispose of the salt you've used for cleansing—don't reuse it for another cleanse. It contains the negative energy it has drawn out of the crystal. (See page 31 though for a note about certain stones that should not be used with salt.)

Tibetan Bells

The sound from the chimes of Tibetan bells retunes crystals and gives them a healing boost. Place the stones on a flat surface and gently ring the bells over the top of them repeatedly.

EMPOWERING YOUR CRYSTAL

After you have cleansed your chosen crystal by using one of the methods on pages 29–32, the next step is to empower it. When you do this, you are making a personal connection with it so that it recognizes your energy and will work its magick alongside you. With this in mind, it's always best to make sure that whoever is casting the spell is the same person who energizes the stone throughout the next steps.

The following procedure must be performed every single time you conduct a spell.

1. **Prepare a quiet room in the house.** Light some candles and dot them around the area where you will be sitting.

2. **Play some beautiful music.** Many kinds of meditation or New Age–style music are available through multiple channels online.

3. **Sit quietly in a chair and cup the crystal in both hands.** Close your eyes and think about the spell you want to perform. Imagine the clear-cut outcome of the spell, and visualize positive energy flowing from you into the stone. Continue with this visualization for at least two minutes.

4. **Speaking out loud, ask the crystal to project its magick.** A short affirmation could go something like this: *"With the magick inside of me, I invite you to release your power to me. Deliver your mighty energy and help me this day."*

5. **Tell the crystal precisely what you want it to do.**

Helpful Examples

If you want to cast a spell to heal someone of ill health, you might say,

*"I ask you to reinforce my magick
and help me to heal {NAME} of their ailments."*

You can even be more specific and tell the crystal exactly what the problem is, saying, for instance:

*"My friend {NAME} is suffering from depression.
I need your help to intensify my magick and bring about a positive outcome.*

*I need them to be free of their emotional pain and to
begin to see the positivity that life can bring."*

You can use the wording above as a guideline, or you might like to use a personal mantra of your own. Some witches like to use repetition and say an incantation over a crystal before a spell begins. You can try the one on the opposite page.

Sample Crystal Incantation

In the evening, place your crystal on a table or worktop and create a ring of salt around it. Circle the salt with seven white tealight candles; light them. This protective circle will shine an invisible light of power directly upward. Stand over the crystal so that your face is directly above the stone. (If you have long hair, please tie it back and be cautious of the flames.) Repeat these words seven times:

"I empower this crystal with magickal light.
I inhale the light this night."

Once you have said the mantra seven times, close by saying, *"So mote it be."*

Chapter 3

The Crystal Toolkit

WHATEVER THE SPELL, WHETHER FROM A BOOK OR concocted on your own, you can always incorporate a crystal into your magick. It's not the case that you have to follow every written spell to the letter. For example, you might find a ritual in a book that doesn't call for a stone, but you can seriously amplify the magick and add to its success if you use a crystal that is related to the problem at hand. For the top twenty essential crystals, see the special color section following on pages 41–52.

CRYSTALS AND CANDLES

When using crystals for magickal purposes, you'll probably want to pull out all the stops to boost your intent, always keeping in mind the Wiccan Rede, which stipulates that spells should not be cast to hurt another person (see page 11). As with all things magickal and spiritual, good intent is key. So how about combining a couple of magickal forces by incorporating candles with your crystal altar, circle, or bed? Whatever layout you choose, candles can emphasize the power you are creating with your stones.

Consider how the flame of a candle brings the facets of a crystal to life in a mystical way. The flickering light shifts, drops, then jumps back to life—the key word being *life*. Candle flame can be a dynamic presence during a spell or meditation. Putting candles together with crystals creates a powerful space for your work. As with all magick and spiritual practice, this is not a hodge-podge process that can be rushed. You are attempting to perform a ritual, and as such, you need to enter into it with consideration, patience, and respect.

Preparing for a Candle-Crystal Ritual

When selecting an appropriate candle for your intended ritual, keep in mind that, once lit, the candle must be allowed to burn to its end (supervised, of course). Consider the size of the candle. Votive candles and tea lights are perfectly acceptable for rituals and are easy to obtain. Want something a little more special? You can purchase spell candles online that were specifically handcrafted for ritualistic purposes.

Before using a store-purchased candle, be sure to cleanse it. This will rid it of any energy that's already "stuck" to it.

There are a few ways to cleanse a candle. A straightforward way to do this is by wiping the candle clean with a cloth, then wetting all but the wick with a warm saltwater solution. While doing this, say,

"This magickal water cleanses thee with good intent and purity."

Another way is to hold the candle by the wick under running water. Pouring pure bottled water or rainwater you previously collected is best. As you cleanse, say the same words:

"This magickal water cleanses thee with good intent and purity."

To assist with your intention, you can take a sharp object, like a small kitchen knife or a hatpin, and etch your name and intention into the wax of the candle. For example:

{YOUR NAME} *Extra money to pay the bills*
or
{NAME} *Stop painful emotions*

Whatever your intention, make sure that you inscribe your wishes clearly. You can cover the candle with your many written desires or use just a few short words.

Anointing

Once you have followed the instructions above, you will need to anoint your candle with oil. There are many different types of oils, all with their own influences, so thoroughly research the various blends. If you are not sure, you can anoint any candle for any spell with pure vegetable oil. This is a good universal oil.

Becoming familiar with a candle before a ritual is similar in practice to the crystal initiation (see pages 23–24). Prepare a peaceful, comfortable space where you will be able to focus on your intention for at least several minutes while holding an unlit candle.

When your candle is properly cleansed, anointed, and initiated, you are ready to perform your ritual. Select the appropriate crystals for the task and lay them upon the altar, near the candle. Light the candle. Say a prayer of gratitude for the crystals' help today. Acknowledge the strength of each stone and thank it for blessing your space. Close your eyes. Breathe deeply, allowing yourself to relax into the aura of the space you've created. Cast your spell, energizing the request with the pure belief that it will come to fruition. Visualize a positive outcome to your application. Open your eyes and gaze upon your crystals, concentrating on their strengths and abilities, especially as they relate to your request. If you like, pick up the various crystals while the candle burns; this will help you connect with their energy directly.

To close the ritual, return the crystals to their place next to the candle (if you picked them up) and take several deep breaths. Open your arms to accept the positive energy you have conjured, so that you may carry it into the coming days as your wish starts to take shape. Bring your hands to your Heart Chakra to seal the energy within your being.

Give a prayer of thanks to your crystals, your candle, the universe, and any spirits you may have invoked.

You may feel worn out after this ceremony, as it is quite compelling, drawing all this energy into one spot. Remember to cleanse and recharge your crystals afterward. You can also shower or bathe with a sea salt rinse to cleanse your own aura.

20
ESSENTIAL
CRYSTALS

ALTHOUGH THERE ARE ENDLESS VARIETIES OF CRYSTALS
on Earth, spellcasters tend to focus on a selection of stones that can
be used in more than one type of spell. Amethyst, for example, has
multiple uses: it helps with many issues such as insomnia, ill health,
and nightmares and is also excellent for meditation. You can use it
over and over in all kinds of spells; it is just one of a few crystals that
many witches find themselves returning to time and again.

Like amethyst, agate, quartz, and a few other semiprecious
stones are staples in every crystal witch's toolkit. In the following
section, we've listed the twenty most commonly used crystals along
with details about them. As you experiment with each of these
crystals (and others), you may find it valuable to make notes about
which stones can be used for what spells in your personal Book of
Shadows. Take account of those that had the best results.

The twenty crystals listed here are tried-and-true essentials that belong in every witch's collection and should be enough to get you started on the path of crystal witchery. For a detailed, comprehensive list of nearly all crystals and their correspondences, see the A–Z Crystal Guide in chapter 4 (pages 57–96).

AGATE

This banded, semiprecious gemstone is a form of
microcrystalline quartz. It cleanses the aura, especially
if a person has suffered emotional trauma. To help settle
painful emotions, lie down and place it over your or your
client's heart. Agate radiates power and calms tempers.
It is also a powerful healing stone; it can help with stomach
and digestive issues and problems with the uterus.

COLOR(S): Common colors include blue, brown, gray, onyx,
and pink; rarer varieties include Botswana, condor, crazy
lace, fire (see below), iris, moss, and plume. OTHER USES: Improves
concentration; helps one to find the truth; promotes self-confidence
and acceptance.

FIRE AGATE

This variety of agate is deep, reddish brown in color and brings
safety and protection to its owner, giving support during
difficult times. It repels negativity, protects from the evil
eye or ill-wishers, and acts as a force field, preventing
negative thoughts from reaching its owner and instead
sending them back to the source. Carry fire agate with you
if you have an enemy or know that someone is thinking ill of you.

COLOR(S): Reddish brown with accents of orange, red, green,
and gold. OTHER USES: Provides support in difficult times; eliminates
cravings and dispels fear.

AMBER

Amber actually isn't a crystal at all; it is fossilized tree resin that has long been valued for its color and beauty. Amber is used widely for healing and for casting out disease from the body. If worn continuously around the throat or wrist, it can balance the chakras and protect against depression or thoughts of suicide. If you are feeling deflated or hopeless, wear amber in the form of a necklace, bracelet, or ring.

COLOR: Golden brown to yellow. **OTHER USES:** Cleanses the environment; brings about stability; enhances wisdom.

AMETHYST

Easily recognizable by its violet hue, this variety of quartz is one of the most potent crystals regularly used by spellcasters. Amethyst combats insomnia and protects against nightmares. It has a beautiful calming effect and can help with meditation or when one would like to tune into a more spiritual vibration. Fretful babies and children react exceptionally well to this stone if it is placed in their bedroom (high up and out of reach for safety, of course).

COLOR: Purple. **OTHER USES:** Aids meditation.

ANGELITE

A variety of *anhydrite* from Peru, this pale blue mineral can assist a witch in powerful healing. As its name suggests, angelite is used primarily for contact and communication with the higher realm. This stone increases telepathic communication, enables astral projection, helps reveal inner truths, and can magickally transform a person's compassion and empathy. Summon an angel every time you cast a spell by placing angelite on your altar.

COLOR(S): Usually blue-flecked with soft white spots, but can alsobe colorless or violet. OTHER USES: Promotes weight control and truth-telling; instills patience and acceptance; stimulates healing of any kind.

AQUAMARINE

A powerful force against all things negative, this greenish-blue semiprecious crystal is a member of the beryl family (see also opposite page, top). It is sometimes carried by sailors as a talisman against drowning. It clears the mind, calms the soul, and is especially good at helping one combat fear. It's also quite effective when entering a nerve-racking situation. Carry aquamarine if you plan to travel over water.

COLOR(S): Greenish blue, but the purest translucent varieties can appear sky blue. OTHER USES: Promotes intelligence and clairvoyant abilities; useful in healing sore throats; soothes during meditation and healing.

BERYL

Beryl encapsulates a large variety of semiprecious crystals, including aquamarine and emerald. This commanding crystal, no matter the variety, deescalates stressful situations and clears away negative energies. It is also an excellent stone for scrying and is often used to create crystal balls. Hold a beryl stone in your hand while performing divination magick, or fix a small piece into your wand.

VARIETIES: Emerald, heliodor, bixbite, aquamarine, maxixe, morganite, and goshenite, among others. **OTHER USES:** Enhances marriages; wards off anxiety and relieves stress; promotes bravery.

BLOODSTONE

Also known as *heliotrope*, this magickal crystal is a variety of jasper with immense power. Weather witches tend to lean toward using this stone, as it was once believed to control weather. Placing this crystal in a small bowl of water by one's bedside will bring restful sleep and sweet dreams. Bloodstone is also a stone of creativity, so it is suitable for any rituals that involve boosting the imagination.

COLOR(S): Dark red, green, or brown, or a combination of the three. **OTHER USES:** Removing ghosts or spirits; repels danger.

CARNELIAN

Carnelian is a semiprecious stone belonging to the chalcedony family. It possesses magickal properties that cleanse and restore other crystals. If placed among other crystals or inside a geode, this brownish-red stone will permeate powerful energies and rid other crystals of contamination. It also works very well for anyone who has been in an abusive situation, providing them with the inner strength to fight back and follow their correct path.

COLOR(S): Red, orange, or brownish-red. **OTHER USES:** Helps with mental preparation for childbirth; thought to influence wealth and abundance; calms angry emotions; puts a stop to mental lethargy.

CELESTITE

Also called *celestine*, this mineral derives its name from the Latin *caelestis*, meaning "celestial" or "heavenly." Naturally, celestite helps its user reach a higher power and connect with the angels and divine guides. Many crystal witches tend to have a piece of this gemstone somewhere nearby when spellcasting.

COLOR(S): Pale blue, pale pink, pale brown, white, yellow, or colorless. **OTHER USES:** Helps heal unhealthy relationships; enhances scrying abilities; removes anxiety and sharpens the mind.

CITRINE

This cheery, bright yellow variety of quartz carries the power of the sun and removes blocks and obstacles from life. Trying to sell your home? You can bury citrine chips in the garden or elsewhere on the property to help speed up the sale.

COLOR(S): Ranges in color from pale to golden yellow, honey-toned shades, or nearly brown.
OTHER USES: Promotes good fortune and success, healing and chakra balancing, wealth, and prosperity; helps heal warring families; enhances concentration; aids with menstrual problems, constipation, and menopause.

FLUORITE

Fluorite is the original fluorescent mineral; it is the inspiration for the term *fluorescence* due to its behavior under ultraviolet light. (To see this in action, let your fluorite sit in bright sunshine for a few minutes, then take it into a dark room. It might glow!) It is a useful stone for protection, drawing out any negativity around a person. It also works as a learning aid, so it is excellent to use in spells that boost mental concentration.

COLOR(S): Translucent purple, yellow, brown, green, or blue; some specimens glow blue-violet under a black light.
OTHER USES: Helps change fixed behavior; calms emotions; encourages reorganization, happiness, and stability in relationships.

MOLDAVITE

Typically forest green in color, this form of tektite is believed to have been formed by a meteorite impact in Europe that took place around 15 million years ago. This stone is intensely powerful and, if the science is accurate, is of extraterrestrial origin. It is so effective that many people describe a feeling of nausea when holding it. Because it is a fragile stone, it is essential that moldavite not be cleansed with salt; it will scratch the surface.

COLOR(S): Forest green, olive green, or bluish green. **OTHER USES**: Enhances psychic abilities and divination; helps heal emotional trauma.

MOONSTONE

Identifiable for its lustrous, opalescent appearance, moonstone is a semiprecious stone associated with the moon and its phases. This crystal is perfect for the cycles and changes that life brings. Worn frequently by psychics, moonstone magnifies intuition and expands the mind.

COLOR(S): Pearly white, cream, blue, yellow, green, or translucent. **OTHER USES**: Aids in emotional healing, menstrual health, and general wellness in women; helps men relate to their feminine side.

ONYX

A variety of chalcedony and a cousin of agate, deep-black onyx brings strength both to the person who needs it and to the spell at hand. It also lends itself well to past-life issues that may be affecting present-day circumstances.

COLOR(S): Black or dark gray, sometimes banded. **OTHER USES:** Gives strength, vigor, and courage; dispels lustful urges; useful in summoning guidance.

QUARTZ

With dozens of varieties and virtually endless uses, quartz is the second-most abundant mineral in Earth's continental crust (after feldspar). It is probably one of the more powerful stones that can be used for magickally unblocking situations. It is an essential healing stone, aligning the chakras and casting out negativity.

MAJOR VARIETIES: Agate, amethyst, carnelian, citrine, jasper, rock crystal, rose, smoky, and tiger's eye, among others. **COLOR(S):** Nearly every color, including colorless. **OTHER USES:** Boosts memory and concentration and unlocks memories; heals deep emotional issues; believed to invigorate the immune system.

ROSE QUARTZ

This popular, pink-hued gemstone is a perfect tool for any type of love, be it *eros* (romantic), *agape* (universal), *storge* (family), *philia* (friendship), or *philautia* (self). Rose quartz is the most frequently used crystal for any ritual pertaining to affairs of the heart.

COLOR(S): Hues of pink. **OTHER USES:** Attracts love; heals relationships; brings about harmonious marriages and unions; helps one to express and release emotions.

TIGER'S EYE

This banded brown gemstone has amazing protective qualities and will repel anyone wishing ill upon you. It is sometimes used by witches to achieve kundalini awakening, or the stirring of the divine energy that lies at the base of the spine. Tiger's eye also improves meditation.

COLOR(S): Brown, red, or yellow; often banded.
OTHER USES: Removes curses and the evil eye; provides protection from anything negative; allows a person to overcome self-doubt and criticism.

TOURMALINE

This stone attunes itself to anything magickal and can eliminate any negativity. Witches like to protect themselves when casting spells and so this stone can be placed on the altar during any ritual.

COLOR(S): Black, brown, gold, green, or pink.
OTHER USES: Heals sadness; helpful in business and promotes happiness.

TURQUOISE

Turquoise, easily recognized by its bright bluish-green color, is a mineral commonly used for protection against danger. It is also thought to change color if infidelity is taking place.

COLOR(S): Light blue, bluish-green, deep green, or blue, some with darker veins or matrices.
OTHER USES: Improves intuition; releases inhibitions; helps one overcome mood swings.

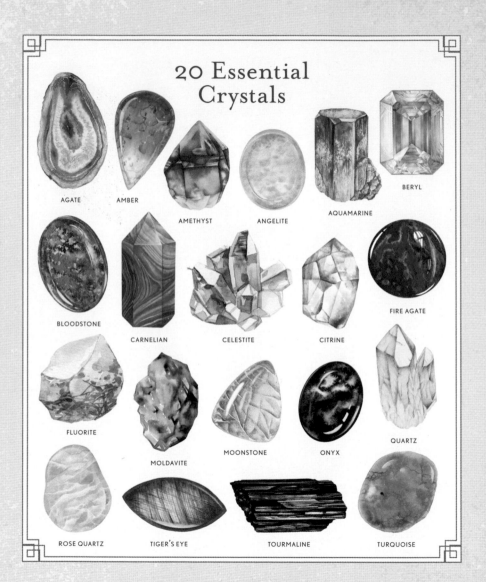

20 Essential Crystals

AGATE

AMBER

AMETHYST

ANGELITE

AQUAMARINE

BERYL

BLOODSTONE

CARNELIAN

CELESTITE

CITRINE

FIRE AGATE

FLUORITE

MOLDAVITE

MOONSTONE

ONYX

QUARTZ

ROSE QUARTZ

TIGER'S EYE

TOURMALINE

TURQUOISE

WHIP UP A CRYSTAL WAND

If you're a fan of a certain young wizard, you've no doubt seen movies in which wands are used to cast all sorts of spells—sometimes with outlandish results! Most witches own a wand. Some buy ready-made ones; others have a go at making their own. If you opt for the latter, apple, willow, hawthorn, and ash are preferred wood choices. When you venture out into nature to collect your branch, always thank the tree afterward. Traditionally, the length of a wood wand should equal the distance from your elbow to the tip of your fingers. Once you've acquired a branch of the appropriate length that is to your liking, you can then sand it down and paint or decorate it however you like.

To incorporate a crystal into your wood wand, hollow out the end and attach a crystal to the tip. It is okay to use glue, but you might prefer craft wire. This will secure the crystal in place, and then you can wind on additional items, like leaves and feathers.

If you decide this is too creative or too much effort, you can purchase a long shard of your preferred crystal to use as a wand. With this option, you can cast aside your big-screen visions of what a wand should look like. Don't worry too much about the size, either. Anything that is long enough to be used as a pointer is fair game.

Once you have either assembled or purchased your wand, you need to familiarize yourself with it. Scrutinize every little detail, touching and feeling the magick growing inside of it.

Wands are sometimes used in feng shui, the practice of the design and arrangement of an environment as it relates to the flow and redirection of energy. For spellcasting, wands are mainly used to cast a circle before a spell begins. (Hold the wand in your right hand and move your arm in a clockwise motion around the altar and its contents. Once your ritual is complete, repeat the movement to close the magickal portal.)

Crystal wands are typically used to move energy when it gets stuck or blocked in the body. Some crystals are perfect for the work associated with crystal wands—quartz and selenite are two popular choices. Quartz is known as a "universal healer" and is useful on auras, chakras, and physical and spiritual ailments. It's an excellent crystal to boost and focus energy, improve relationships, and increase psychic abilities. Selenite, meanwhile, promotes insight and clarity, boosts positive energy in your surroundings, and can assist in forging relationships with spiritual beings.

Both quartz and selenite are known for their ability to acclimate and work well with almost any person's energy. And despite how hard these crystals work, they don't need to be cleansed all that often—they're both beauty and brawn! Of course, quartz and selenite are mere suggestions, especially for anyone who has never worked with a wand—there are heaps of other crystals to choose from, depending on what your intention is.

Wand Practice

Because wands are used in the movement of energy, they are often used in practice with clients, but you can certainly use one to clear your own trouble spots as well. Knowing a little about chakras is helpful in this practice. Here is a quick reference guide to the auras and the focus of each for those who may not be familiar:

ROOT Positioned at the base of the spine; helps one feel grounded; aids in issues surrounding everyday well-being, like shelter, food, and safety

SACRAL Found in the lower abdomen/pelvic area; heightens acceptance, allowing one to open up to new people and experiences; focuses on sexuality and gratification in life

SOLAR PLEXUS Located in the navel/lower torso; impacts confidence, self-esteem, and personal well-being

HEART Found in the center of the chest; concentrates on love, peace, and delights in life

THROAT Centered in the throat; a source of communication and the ability to express oneself

THIRD EYE Located in the center of the brow; supports intuition, wisdom, and focus

CROWN Found at the top of the head; the highest chakra; enables one's connection to their spiritual self

Chakra comes from the Sanskrit word for "wheel," which describes these centers of energy. They usually spin peacefully, processing and moving energy through the body. Sometimes energy can get trapped along the way, and this manifests in emotional or spiritual issues. For example, it may feel like you can't do anything right, you're making mistakes at work, and your relationship is at sixes and sevens, and you're not sure how to fix any of it. In this case, your Root Chakra might be blocked and in need of an energetic clearing with a crystal wand.

To clear blocked chakra energy, try holding the tip of your wand just above the affected chakra. Gently, with a pulling or scooping motion, direct the energy away from that spot. Visualize that you are either moving the negative energy along a path or lifting it up and out of the body. Imagine that you're releasing the blockage, allowing it to flow freely and disperse.

You can try this with any painful spot on the body as well (but if the pain persists, make sure to follow up with your doctor).

Chapter 4

The A–Z
Crystal Guide

CRYSTALS ARE EVERYWHERE; EACH ONE HOLDS THE POWER to energize your intentions. In Part One, we provided you with a list of the most commonly used crystals, some of which a witch might have in her magickal collection. In this section, we're going to explore the application of crystals from a broader perspective. The comprehensive crystal list on the following pages is a must-have for anyone wanting to practice Wicca. You will be able to see at a glance which stones are suitable for any spell you might like to cast. After confirming your choice, jump online and look up the stone so you can see an image of it. That way, when you venture out to purchase the crystal, you'll have some idea of what it looks like. At the end of this long list is an additional reference guide in which you can see crystals grouped by issue (see pages 91–96).

Remember, you can incorporate any of the associated crystals with any rituals that you might want to perform. Placing a stone on your altar will only give the spell more weight and encourage a successful outcome. Crystals also work brilliantly as a charm or talisman after a spell has been cast; you can wear or hold them when the need arises. Just follow the guidelines in the previous chapters and make sure you cleanse, charge, and empower your stone prior to any ritual use. If you find that a stone works well in one of your spells, make sure that you write it in your personal Book of Shadows so that you can refer to it later.

Take it from us: there are so many crystals and gemstones in this world that if you get the crystal bug, you'll spend a lifetime collecting them.

– A –

ADAMITE Promotes happiness, creativity, and love; raises positive energy; used in spells for communication

AEGIRINE Provides protection from dark energy; promotes positive energy

AFGHANITE Helps with any kind of problem-solving

AGATE Protects and soothes; promotes confidence

> **Blue lace** Encourages communication, insight, self-assuredness, calm, and peace; used for healing; helps calm argumentative children and settle the emotions of a parent
>
> **Botswana** Inspires creativity, transitions, solution-seeking; eases feelings of loneliness, grief, and loss
>
> **Crab fire** Gives courage, individual spirit; eases pain in the lower back and reproductive areas
>
> **Crazy lace** Protects against the evil eye; promotes insight and focus in decision-making
>
> **Carnelian (banded)** Helps children with low self-esteem
>
> **Dendritic** Boosts insight and confidence found in spiritualism

Ellensburg blue Clears the Throat Chakra, promotes communication

Eye Provides protection from ill-wishers and the evil eye

Fire Brings passion to a relationship; used in spells involving sexuality, vibrant spirituality, creativity, and focused intention

Holly blue Helps unleash psychic abilities; manifests a spiritual intention

Moss Offers grounding, strength, determination

Purple sage Good for aura cleansing, healing, persistence, and spiritual connections

AGNITITE Aids in perseverance, transition, spiritual cleansing; good for healing rituals

AJOITE Used in love spells, spiritual restoration, emotional stability, and connection with angels

ALBITE For any kind of spiritual work; boosts psychic powers

ALEXANDRITE Balances unhappy emotions; provides confidence and self-esteem; a general stone used for luck and success

Crystal Facts: Alexandrite

This stone was first mined in Russia in the seventeenth century and was named for Czar Alexander II. It is a very unusual stone that will appear to be different colors depending on the light in which it's viewed, from blue-green-yellow in the daytime to pink-red in the evening. A single carat of Alexandrite can cost tens of thousands of dollars! If worn, this jewel heightens self-esteem and brings about good fortune.

AMAZONITE Heals physical ailments, so excellent for spells to bring about better health

AMBER Dissipates negative energy and removes any kind of fear; attracts luck and balances emotions; good for environmental cleansing and enhancing wisdom

AMBLYGONITE Unlocks psychic energy, releases stress, and helps one break away from emotional ties

AMEGREEN Aids in spiritual peace and healing; increases sympathy, kindness, and insight

AMETHYST Helps improve insomnia and banish nightmares; can be used in healing any kind of ailment; animals also respond well to amethyst

AMETHYST-CACOXENITE May help remove painful memories from childhood or past lives

AMETRINE Removes negativity from the aura; brings about clarity and understanding

AMMOLITE Has great healing abilities; particularly good for fighting depression

ANDALUSITE Blocks negativity; use as a protective stone for people and houses

ANDESINE Relieves stress

ANGELITE For peace and connecting with angels; helps promote sleep

APATITE Used to control weight loss

Blue Enhances insight and psychic abilities; removes blockages and obstacles from life

Golden Improves imagination and focus; gives insight and helps one achieve goals

Green Is used in spells to heal long-term illnesses

APOPHYLLITE

Clear Heals emotional wounds and helps recovery from past events; opens the soul to other spiritual and psychic planes

Green Is used in all spells connected to nature

AQUAMARINE
Controls tempers and relieves stress; good to use to lessen obstinance or anger

ARAGONITE

Blue Good for working with divination, as it brings perception and insight and helps psychic connections

Spanish Increases energy and lessens lethargy

Star clusters Removes residual energy from buildings and houses; a good stone for home cleansing

ASTROPHYLLITE
Is used for making correct decisions

AVENTURINE
A type of quartz, effective in fertility rituals

Blue Helps with self-restraint and control

Green (common) A good stone to carry when taking exams, as it increases intelligence; boosts cash flow; can be used to bring about change in career, find a new job, or get a promotion; encourages strength after surgery

Red Renowned for being the stone of good luck; kept in cash boxes to increase money; can also aid passion

AXINITE
Good for overall health and combatting faults; improves physical energy, so often used in healing spells

AZEZTULITE™
Recently discovered in the United States, part of the quartz family; a powerful shielding stone said to keep one safe; for connection with solar gods and power; use in any spells that call for protection; also works well with citrine for moving to a new house

Amazez Thought to be helpful to people fighting cancer

Black Can be used in spells to alleviate chronic health problems; gives the sick positivity for healing

Golden Enhances about astral travel and projection; practice meditating with this stone nearby

Pink For all things relating to love and emotional stability

Red fire Improves vigor, wisdom, passion, endurance, and psychic/visualization abilities

AZUMAR™ Brings peace and pleasure

AZURITE Thought to increase intelligence and wisdom; opens the mind to all things spiritual

– B –

BARITE Encourages spiritual awareness; enables astral travel and projection; improves intuitive abilities

BASTNÄSITE Can bring dreams into reality

BENITOITE For psychic enhancement and channeling of energies; heightens intuition; can be used in healing, especially in directing good energy toward those with blood disorders

BERYL Gives strength when dealing with stress and removes emotional baggage; used also to boost scrying techniques; an overall good healing stone; many colors and varieties, see also Aquamarine, Emerald, Goshenite, Heliodor, Morganite

Red Encourages inner strength if used in ritual magick

BERYLLONITE Brings happiness, joy, and alignment with the universe and the divine

BIXBITE Arouses passions and improves one's sex life; helps with courage and self-love

Crystal Facts: Red Beryl

This stone is found in Utah, usually in pieces that are too small for jewelers to work with. If you own a show-worthy piece, it can sell for approximately $10,000 per carat!

BLOODSTONE Helpful when dealing with relationship issues; brings love in difficult situations and boosts vigor, healing, courage, and determination

BOJI™ STONE Helps heal painful joints; sold in pairs; can be used as healing stones in spellcraft

BOWENITE Excellent for those moving to a new house; offers a clear way forward while leaving negative issues behind; can also be used for protection and dream interpretation

BRAZILIANITE Enhances determination; good for motivation

BRONZITE Protects at the highest level, sends negative energy back to the sender

BROOKITE Enhances communication between spirits and souls, and an opening of the higher-level chakras

BUSTAMITE Attracts creativity and joy and clears blocked energies

– C –

CACOXENITE A positive stone that raises the vibrations of other crystals around it; releases toxic energies and purifies the spirit and soul

CALCITE Has different uses depending on the color

> **Black (Shamanite)** Raises vibrations and connection to a higher plane; cleanses those with negativity stuck to their aura

> **Blue** Clears negative energies from its environment; use in house blessings

> **Clear** Enhances insight and wisdom; promotes compassion and understanding

Crystal Facts: Brazilianite

This brilliant yellow-green stone was named for Brazil, its country of origin, where it was discovered in the 1940s. Brazil is the largest producer of topaz, amethyst, and aquamarine in the world. Citrine is also abundant there, as well as in Bolivia, Uruguay, and Argentina.

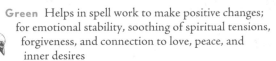

Green Helps in spell work to make positive changes; for emotional stability, soothing of spiritual tensions, forgiveness, and connection to love, peace, and inner desires

Honey Is used for any kind of intellectual pursuits; excellent to give to youngsters taking tests and exams

Merkabite Removes blockages and obstructions, both from life and from the chakras; used for enlightenment and spiritual expansion, astral travel and projection, and high-level spiritual pursuits

Orange Good for summoning new ideas and removing mental blockages; used for sexuality, courage, confidence, and creativity

Pink, opaque Associated with the angels; promotes comfort, security, health, safety, and compassion

Pink, transparent Used for spiritual well-being and restoration; invokes peace and happiness

Red Helps with any kind of learning, as it develops the senses and insight

CARNELIAN Has the capability to cleanse other crystals; can be used to protect the house and home (if placed near the front door, it will invite abundance); contains powerful healing energies and is especially good for combatting arthritis; commonly used in fertility spells

CASSITERITE Helps when suffering against prejudice, rejection, or unfairness, as it helps to dissolve these emotions

CATLINITE Connects user to spiritual beings through prayer and ritual communication

CAVANSITE Develops and enhances psychic abilities and spiritual perception; allows one the freedom to change their mind-set

CELESTITE (Celestine) Is used for communication with angels and spirit guides and for any form of scrying or divination, and sends healing energy for eye and ear disorders; brings light and love into the home when on display (do not place in direct sunlight, as it will fade)

CHALCANTHITE Removes obstacles that delay progress; good to use when waiting for something to arrive or when trying to sell one's home

CHALCEDONY Has different uses depending on the color (*chalcedony* is also a general term for the many varieties of microcrystalline quarts such as bloodstone, carnelian, chrysoprase, jasper, moss agate, and onyx)

> Blue Casts out worries and fears and brings a sense of optimism

> Purple Offers spiritual and auric cleansing, enhancement of psychic abilities, and connection with high-level spirituality

CHALCOPYRITE Uplifts one's mood and clears away energy blockages; removes nervousness, so good to carry into interviews or when speaking publicly

CHAROITE Works well for providing emotional healing to those who are lonely or who live alone

CHRYSOBERYL Enhances psychic dreams and vision and protects from evil and the evil eye; inspires forgiveness; use this crystal for self-control, especially when trying to lose weight; also effective for any kind of learning or studying

CHRYSOCOLLA Helps calm rocky relationships and achieve balance and peace

CHRYSOPRASE Can help people suffering from melancholy; manifests optimism and joy; place by homegrown herbs or vegetables to boost production

CITRINE Prevents obstacles and blockages in life; often used in rituals when moving to a new house; attracts wealth and prosperity, fosters self-esteem and confidence, and reduces anger

CLINOCHLORE Connects user to spiritual beings and planes; offers peace, strength, and clarification of spiritual goals

COOKEITE Can be used in office environments to clear away frenzied energies; good for spells to bring about better success at work

CORUNDUM See Ruby and Sapphire

COVELLITE (Covelline) Assists with psychic development, spiritual awakening, insight, perception, and connection to a higher spiritual plane

CREEDITE Perfect for getting over a lost love or any kind of bad relationship; for spiritual enhancement and communication with the universe and divine powers

CUPRITE Increases healing, strength, and physical stamina; raises energy levels; focuses on masculine energy; treats problems with willpower; dispels worries and concerns, giving clarity of mind

– D –

DANBURITE Magickally removes anxiety and worry; works best in spells to alleviate sadness

   Agni gold Is used for spiritual insight and receiving spiritual messages; improves joy, integrity, and telepathic powers

DARWIN GLASS Enhances and improves relationships; can also be used for spells that call for humanity and altruism

DATOLITE A must-have stone for solving almost any problem; particularly useful in dealing with difficult neighbors

DESERT ROSE (crystal clusters of gypsum or barite) Empowers and helps one stand their ground in difficult circumstances; for intuition and mental calm

DIAMOND Shines like a light of positivity, removing fears and emotional upsets; also boosts vitality, passion, and creativity (See Crystal Facts, opposite page)

DIASPORE Increases memory power and stimulates focus; can be used to bring about emotional clarity and strength

DIOPSIDE Is used for love magick, to open the heart and receive love; can also be used in spells to find the truth

   Black star Brings happiness into life

   Chrome Works as a guardian, with strong protective properties

DIOPTASE Promotes empathy, kindness, forgiveness, understanding, and a realignment of energetic patterns

Crystal Fact: Diamonds

The word *diamond* comes from the ancient Greek word *adamas*, meaning "unbreakable," and diamonds are indeed the hardest naturally occurring material on Earth.

They are the traditional gemstone for marriage, and many couples learn about the four *C*s (cut, clarity, color, and carat) when looking for engagement rings. The stone is not as rare as you might think—it is the most commonly owned stone, and according to some gemologists, one of the most common gems in nature.

Russia is the world's largest producer of rough diamonds by volume, while Botswana is the second largest producer and the leading country in terms of value. Western Australia is the world's largest producer of color diamonds by volume. In ancient Greece and Rome, people thought diamonds were tears from the gods or pieces of fallen stars. The Romans also believed that the tip of Cupid's arrow was made from this sparkling stone, which could explain why it is associated with love and marriage. In the Middle Ages, folks believed diamonds had curative properties.

The world's largest and most expensive diamond is the Cullinan I, or Great Star of Africa. It weighs 530.2 carats and is part of the Crown Jewels of the United Kingdom. Its value could be up to $2 billion! The second-most expensive diamond is the 45.5 carat Hope Diamond (shown in a nineteenth-century engraving of one of the crown jewels of France, right—the stone is set at the bottom), and once owned by King Louis XIV and renowned for its rare, blue color. It is valued at approximately $300 million. The diamond's famous curse was likely a nineteenth-century story that was embellished to spark interest in the stone.

A planet made almost entirely of carbon was recently discovered —and one-third of it is pure diamond. Can you imagine living there?

Crystal Facts: Emeralds

This vibrant green stone has been held in high esteem for four thousand years and was a favorite of none other than Cleopatra, who wore them as a sign of wealth and power. Emeralds were also thought to promote fertility, immortality, and future-telling.

Because of their soothing color, emeralds were used in Ancient Greece to treat and prevent eyestrain. In the Middle Ages, they were used to treat various illnesses, including demon possession!

Emeralds are softer than diamonds and can be chipped and scratched. This is because they can have inclusions, materials trapped inside the stone, such as other crystals or liquid. These are technically imperfections but are often referred to as *jardins* ("gardens" in French).

Emeralds are a variety of the mineral beryl—the same material that forms aquamarine. Columbia has a rich supply of emeralds and is the world's largest producer.

DOLOMITE Is used for grounding, mindfulness, and emotional and spiritual stability; can also be used in spells to help with patience

DRAVITE From the tourmaline family; good for emotional stability, mindfulness, understanding, and patience

DRUZY (any rock coated with fine crystals) Helps the owner feel more relaxed; used in spells to combat melancholy

DUMORTIERITE Provides focus, intellectual enhancement, motivation and creativity, and psychic visions

– E –

EILAT STONE (King Solomon stone) Banishes anything negative and removes painful memories; also used in spells for communication

EMERALD Brings abundance, love, domestic bliss, empathy, understanding, and repairing the mind and soul with emotional healing; can also be used in friendship spells and for anything romantic

ENHYDRO CRYSTAL (quartz with water-filled cavity) Reduces tension in relationships, both platonic and romantic

EPIDOTE Removes negative energy and blockages from one's life; changes energy from negative to positive

EUCLASE Brings about happiness and improves intuition

EUDIALYTE Promotes self-compassion and manifestation; can magickally enhance personal power, leaving one feeling more motivated

– F –

FLUORITE Defends against bad dreams; brings about decisiveness and cleans energy; can be used in fertility spells and for protection against negative people

   Magenta Enhances focus on the Heart Chakra, integrity of the spirit and soul, and higher planes of consciousness

FUCHSITE Offers emotional stability and calmness of the spirit; can be used in spells to bring about changes of any kind and for new beginnings

FULGURITE Is used for spiritual focus, expression of purpose, and intent; can be used to connect with divine energy

– G –

GABBRO Good for any kind of healing energy related to the cardiovascular system; helps with grounding, maintaining spiritual stability during times of transformation

GAIA STONE (from 1980 Mount St. Helens eruption) Is used in spells to connect to the divine goddess energy; enhances relationships with the earth and nature; also encourages prosperity and cash flow

GALAXITE Used in rituals to master the art of astral projection; balances the aura, heals, and cleanses

GALENA Helps in discovering past lives, restoration of the soul, self-discovery, and transformation

GARNET Varying uses depending on the color/variety

    Almandine Offers safety, power, protection, and well-being; brings strength and power, so good for empowering one's self

    Black andradite Attracts romance and intimacy

    Green Provides strength and abundance; enhances manifestation power

    Grossularite Can be used for a positive outcome with challenging lawsuits; enhances fertility

    Red Promotes love and passion; commonly used in love magick

    Rhodolite Aids in self-healing; helps overcome frigidity

    Spessartine Suppresses nightmares

GASPÉITE A wonderful healing stone that must be worn; the longer you wear it, the more powerful the healing becomes

GOETHITE Soothes grief, helps emotional healing, and boosts creativity and vision; enhances one's relationship to nature

GOLDSTONE Enhances power, motivation, and determination; boosts confidence and positivity

GOSHENITE Used in spells for communication with angels, spirits, and spirit guides

– H –

HACKMANITE Helps one feel true to themselves; can be used during deep meditations

    Blue A cleansing stone; can be used to eliminate negative energies and improve psychic ability

    Pink Brings peace to problematic situations

HALITE Promotes happiness and feelings of wellbeing; also used for enhancing mindfulness and psychic awareness

HANKSITE Advances one's spiritual side; aids meditation

HELIODOR Seems to shine with the light of the sun; brings success and happiness

HEMATITE Many uses: good for legal situations; helps fainthearted women become stronger; improves willpower; heightens memory and concentration; effective with anything educational; brings about a better night's sleep; effective with house blessings and removing warts

    Rainbow Offers safety and protection from negative energy

HEMIMORPHITE Improves communication with loved ones; intensifies connections with angels; brings about happiness and joy

HERDERITE Used for focus on brightness and lightness of being; sharpens the mind, aids in learning

HEULANDITE Helps with mending emotions and relieves emotional burdens; useful for dream enhancement and lucid dreaming

HIDDENITE Attracts love and repairs relationships; nurses and supports a broken heart; can be used to bring about success at work

HOWLITE Helps dissolve stress, anxiety, and fear

HYPERSTHENE Helps achieve one's goals in any aspect of life

— I —

IOLITE Can be used alongside mediation and visualization; helps with astral travel, inner journeying, and focus

IRONSTONE Eliminates negative energies

-J-

JADE (Jadeite and Nephrite) Effective in fertility rituals and anything connected to reproductive organs; used in spells to combat insomnia; for emotional stability, protection of the spirit, and love

Black Offers protection; best used to repel negative energy and fight against hauntings and demonic entities

Blue Calms; used to bring about peace and clarity

Green Has a variety of uses: draws in good luck and abundance; can be used as a protective stone, promoting peace and serenity; used in spells to cement or attract new friendships

Lavender Connects user with angels and heightens spiritual vibration

Purple Promotes happiness and lightness of being, insight, wisdom, compassion, and humor

Crystal Facts: Jade

The first mining of jade in China dates as far back as Neolithic times. Considered the imperial gem of China, the stone was used throughout Asia for objects of all types, from practical tools and decorative items to intricate artworks and ceremonial pieces.

There are two species of jade: jadeite, which ranges from white to deep green as well as many other colors; and nephrite, in colors from white, to yellow, brown, and green. Imperial jade (jadeite), with its vivid, rich green color, is considered the most valuable and can cost about $30,000 per ounce.

This stone is used magickally for helping to ease kidney problems and anything connected to the reproductive organs.

JASPER Increases physical strength and endurance; helps one deal with difficult situations; for communicating with pets

   Black (Basanite) Absorbs bad energies; soaks up negativity in the home

    Brecciated Supports healing spells; also effective in money and work rituals

     Dalmatian Brings playfulness and happiness to life; the black spots found in this variety is black tourmaline, which makes it excellent for protection

      Fancy Helps broken hearts; promotes creativity and self-restraint

      Kambaba (crocodile) Boosts plant growth; reduces anxiety when rubbed repeatedly; banishes nightmares and terrors by eliminating negativity

      King cobra Nurtures the spirit; dissolves resentment and anger

      Leopard skin Protects against negativity

      Mookaite Is thought to slow the aging process; gives for connection with the earth; boosts peace of mind and joy

      Ocean Brings abundance and gratitude; manifests positive intent; dissolves negative energy

      Picture Alleviates fears and anxiety; brings about a sense of calm

     Poppy Improves relationships with animals; brings joy into life

    Rathbunite Helps with creativity and pleasure

  Red Promotes independence and self-determination; for love and passion, balancing energies, and physical well-being

  Spider Boosts connection with the universe; calms frayed nerves and eases stress; helps remove spiders from the home

  Unakite Effective in love spells for lasting relationships

  Yellow Focuses on the Solar Plexus Chakra, for clearing and strengthening

JET Aids in grounding, safety, and cleansing; releases grief; boosts financial security and protection

JEREMEJEVITE Rare; helps with any kind of divination

– K –

KINOITE Enhances telepathic abilities; promotes loyalty, fidelity, and communication

KUNZITE Promotes emotional cleansing and balancing; connects with the universe and divine energy; decreases stress and heals broken hearts

KYANITE Is used for grounding, boosting telepathy, astral travel, connection with other planes, and time travel; does not absorb negative energy so rarely needs cleansing

> **Blue** Supports retrieval of past-life details, telepathic powers, and compassion
>
> **Green** Connects practitioner with nature and Earth
>
> **Orange** Offers focus on Sacral Chakra cleansing and balancing, passion and sexuality, creative thought and behavior, and manifestation
>
> **Indigo** Bolsters intuition and spiritual visions, lucid dreaming, astral projection, enlightenment, and spiritual evolution

– L –

LABRADORITE Thought to encourage protection from negative energy; believed to amplify any ritual; helps with insomnia

> **Golden** Balances energy

LAPIS LAZULI Works well in truth spells (see Crystal Facts, opposite page)

LARIMAR Offers calm and metaphysical soothing, communication, and connection to feminine energies; used for healing

LAZULITE Reduces frustration; soothes migraines and headaches; boosts lucid dreaming

LAZURITE Stimulates memory

LEPIDOCROCITE Repairs an injured soul and emotions; used in spells to encourage calm in those suffering from attention-deficit/hyperactivity disorder or autism spectrum disorder

LEPIDOLITE Stress-busting stone; stone used for physical and emotional wellness and peace of mind, boosts meditation

LODESTONE (Magnetic magnetite; see Magnetite) Helps attract what one desires

Crystal Facts: Ancient Egyptians

Ancient Egyptians were among the first peoples to adorn themselves with colorful stones and, with precious metals, such as gold. They believed that blue was a particularly royal and protective color. As a result, lapis lazuli and turquoise were two of their most coveted stones.

Not only was jewelry worn as a status symbol; it was also thought to protect against evil spirits. Because of their heightened superstition, the Egyptians would wear crystals set into amulets, necklaces, collars, pendants, rings, and other creations to ward off dark entities. They also carried these beliefs to the grave and buried their dead with protective stones not only so the jewels could be enjoyed in the afterlife, but also to ensure that their loved ones made it safely through the underworld.

A prime example of this can be seen in King Tutankhamun's gold burial mask and collar from c. 1323 BCE, which contains inlaid lapis lazuli, along with obsidian, turquoise, quartz, and carnelian, among other stones.

MAGNESITE Helps when drastic changes in life are needed; for inner vision, bliss, and euphoria of the soul

MAGNETITE Aids in grounding and developing new skills

MALACHITE Helps heal a broken heart and dispel fears; influences financial abundance; has protective properties, especially when traveling

MAORI GREENSTONE A type of nephrite used by the Maori people as a protection amulet; also eases depression; see also Jade/Nephrite

MARCASITE Enhances meditation; brings courage when used as a talisman

MERLINITE (Dendritic agate) Brings good luck

MOLDAVITE Powerful, and extraterrestrial; increases psychic abilities; removes blocks and obstacles

MOONSTONE Improves intuition, any form of magick or mysticism, dream activation, lucid dreaming, and calm sleep; invites companionship and friendship in one's life

    Rainbow Used in spells alongside moon magick; helps bring positivity when life is hard

MORGANITE Connects its user to divine energy and the universe; releases burdens and heals emotional wounds

MUSCOVITE Improves psychic abilities and boosts mental power; effective in spells for improving intellect

MUSGRAVITE Enhances healing rituals to ease symptoms

– N –

NATROLITE Creates magickal altar water when placed in water for a few minutes

NUUMITE For magickal intention, self-reflection, self-determination, and growth; energizes the chakras and helps a person connect to the universe

– O –

OBSIDIAN Can be used for a wide range of situations depending on the variety

  Apache tears For grounding, spiritual protection, and spiritual restoration; good to have beside the bed at night; children react well to this crystal, especially if they are feeling sad or hopeless

  Black Provides protection from psychic attack; removes, blocks, or banishes negative people or entities; grounds and heals its user

  Gold sheen Boosts personal power, stopping anyone or anything from controlling you

  Mahogany Brings confidence, unlocking your hidden abilities

  Peacock Encourages astral projection

  Rainbow Attracts love and new relationships

  Snowflake Dissolves harmful thoughts and removes negativity

This is another relatively recently discovered stone, first mined in 1967 in the Musgrave Ranges in South Australia. There have been findings of this gem in other areas of the world such as Antarctica, Greenland, Tanzania, and Myanmar, but those are usually small in quantity.

This stone is so rare and hard to find, that it has sold for $35,000 per carat in the past. It was recently officially renamed magnesiotaaffeite-6N'3S.

OKENITE Keeps undesirable people from entering your life; a cleansing stone used for angelic communication

OLIVINE Used to raise energies and promote patience; see also Peridot

ONYX Guards against the evil eye; brings peace during childbirth

OPAL

Black precious Strengthens the character and balances emotions

Blue Peruvian Good for self-esteem, self-expression, and soothing anxiety and fear

Common Enhances willpower; good to wear if trying to lose weight

Fire, Mexican fire Promotes loyalty and fidelity; brings good luck, likelihood of wealth, and more fluid relationships

Oregon Used in meditation to explore past lives; for creativity, happiness, and expression of the spirit

Owyhee blue Used to summon the highest spiritual protection

Pink Peruvian Encourages the release of past traumas; attracts love, romance, and kindness

Violet flame Promotes distance from negativity

White precious Stabilizes and protects the spirit

OPALITE Improves communication

ORTHOCLASE Helps lift and lighten heavy energy

Crystal Facts: Olivine

Olivine is a common mineral, mostly crystallized from volcanic magma. The translucent, gem-quality version of the stone is called *peridot*. It is mostly mined in Norway. In June 2018, locals on the Big Island of Hawai'i near the Kilauea volcano began finding miniature green grains of olivine near the volcano eruption site, and speculated that they had fallen from the sky after the eruption. Experts later confirmed that the crystals were not related to the eruption but were from beach erosion.

Crystal Facts: Opals

Until recently, most opals, regardless of type, were mined in Australia, but in recent years Ethiopia has become a major producer. Opals are also mined in smaller quantities elsewhere, including in Nevada and Idaho in the United States, as well as in Mexico and Peru.

They can be used as powerful healing stones. Black opals are also called dark opals. They are like traditional opals but contain light-colored streaks on a dark body color.

Peru is home to the somewhat rare Peruvian opal. It's the country's national stone and forms only in the Andes Mountains. Peruvian opals can have a blue or pink hue and are less iridescent than classic opals. Legend has it that they promote relaxation and communication.

– P –

PAINITE Believed to be connected to the planets, it draws in energy from the universe to heal

PAPAGOITE May ease the suffering of grief; brings about more optimism

PERIDOT Used in magick to invoke money, happiness, and prosperity

PETALITE Dispels negativity

PHENAKITE For psychic vision, inner awakenings, third-eye stimulation, and astral travel

Crystal Facts: Painite

Mineralogist Arthur C. D. Pain first discovered this gem in Myanmar in the 1950s. Until 2001, there were only three known specimens of the stone. Since then, there have been other discoveries of Painite, but it's still exceedingly rare and sells for $50,000 to $60,000 per carat.

PIEMONTITE Promotes self-healing and optimism

PIETERSITE Helps one find solutions to problems

PLANCHEITE Boosts courage during difficult times

PREHNITE Associated with archangel Raphael; connects user to the spiritual vibration

PROUSTITE Releases negative energy; for connection to nature

PROPHECY STONE Furthers psychic vision

PURPURITE Helps one speak out and not be afraid; works well in spells when you need to ask for a pay raise or be more assertive

PYRITE Provides protection from physical danger or environmental pollution; used widely in money rituals to increase cash

PYROMORPHITE Boosts the power of other stones in its vicinity

– Q –

QUARTZ Has many uses depending on variety; thought to be the most powerful amplifying stone, giving all stones in its vicinity a lift

Anandalite Offers spiritual enlightenment, insight, imagination, and visualization

Angel aura For use in spells pertaining to the physical body; soothes and calms, bringing enlightenment and creative thought

Angel phantom (Amphibole) Used for connecting user to angels and one's highest spiritual self; used in meditation for angelic communication

Black phantom Used for moving on from the past and restoration of the soul and spirit; helps one reclaim lost or damaged energy; for spiritual strength, determination, and courage

Blue Calms the mind and eradicates fears

Cathedral (Lightbrary) Promotes enlightenment; opens the mind to higher levels of the spirit and development of spiritual goals

Celestial (candle) Aids in spiritual grounding and acceptance of spiritual knowledge and messages

Clear Leaves energy in a perfect state, especially in homes; good to have on the altar during any kind of spellcasting; works as a perfect companion to meditation; helps bring about peaceful sleep; used for connecting telepathically to animals

Columbian dream Soothes; for recovery of dream information, a boost of dream power, lucid dreaming, astral projection, and a link to spirit guides; use in spells for a better night's sleep

Eisen (hematoid) Is used for mischievousness of the spirit, light-heartedness, self-love, brightness, positivity, and enthusiasm

Elestial Offers focus of energy from mystical realms and for grounding

Faden Harmonizes the aura; helps heal emotional wounds and promotes physical well-being

Green Inspires creativity

Harlequin Thought to increase one's ability to overcome illness; works to improve the memory

Hollandite Sharpens intuition and spiritual insight; projects positive energy to help one achieve goals

Imperial gold Aids self-control, willpower, emotional stability, and strength

Isis (five-sided) Named after the Egyptian goddess Isis; for protective spells pertaining to nature

Lemon Strengthens communication

Lithium Enhances serenity, harmony, and dissolution of negative energy; helps rid a person of depression

Moldau Maintains positive energy in the body; should be used after a time of stress or ill health

Molybdenite Gives perseverance, strength, courage, grounding, and mindfulness

Nirvana (Himalayan ice) Good for deep meditation

Prasiolite Aids a person's spiritual development

Rainbow Scatters healing energy through the body

Rose Aids in romance, love, friendships, or anything to do with relationships in general; promotes fertility; a healing stone

Ruby aura For passion and inner strength

Russian red Used to spice up one's love life, excitement, and sexuality

Rutilated Magnifies the power of other crystals

Seriphos green Connects user with nature; offers healing; leaves a person with a sense of good health

Siberian blue Quiets a busy mind and promotes clear thinking; used in nature rituals for animals and wildlife

Sichuan Used for chakra balancing and healing

Smoky Amplifying; used to clear negative energy; helps calm fractious relationships

Spirit (cactus) Aids in connecting with the spirit world or accessing anything mystical

Tangerine Brings about harmonious situations; good for passion and sex

Tanzan aura Amplifies insight, wisdom, and psychic vision

Titanium Brings peace, harmony, abundance, and amplification of positive energy; raises the spiritual energies; good to use alongside divination

Tibetan black Energy- and chakra-cleansing; creates a shield against negativity

White phantom Spiritually and energetically cleansing; for mystical knowledge

Witches finger Used in spells for protection and to overcome fear

– R –

RHODIZITE Amplifies power of other crystals; enhances psychic abilities and emotional strength

RHODOCROSITE Attracts romance and helps heal broken hearts

RHODONITE Very good in spells for decision-making, especially where love is concerned; and for spells to conceive a child

RHYOLITE Used to help people connect and communicate with animals and nature

> **Rainforest jasper** Aids in Earth-healing rituals and the protection of wildlife; restores spiritual faith when lost
> **New Zealand (Mount Paku, marketed as Pakulite)** Used in spells for passion and sexuality; inspires the creative mind

RUBELLITE For commitment to a new beginning or fresh start; see Tourmaline

RUBY Gives determination, strength, passion, boldness, excitement, devotion, and prosperity

Crystal Facts: Rubies

The word *ruby* comes from the Latin *ruber*, meaning "red." This stone is the second-hardest material on Earth (tied with sapphire). Rubies are found in Asia and Southeast Asia (the highest quality ones in Myanmar and Sri Lanka), the United States, Australia, and Africa—specifically in Kenya, Mozambique, Madagascar, Tanzania, and Kenya. Rubies are thought to bring power and protection to those who wear them. (Remember Dorothy's ruby-red slippers in *The Wizard of Oz*?) They are also associated with love and passion due to their vibrant red hue.

In ancient times, warriors and soldiers wore rubies into battle; it was believed that a ruby would darken when danger was approaching.

Larger rubies of exceptional dark, purplish-red color sell for more than similarly sized diamonds, as they are much rarer. Rubies and sapphires are both made of the mineral corundum. The only difference between these gems is their color, caused by different trace elements in the stone (chromium is what makes rubies red).

RUBY FUCHSITE Enhances self-esteem, confidence, and power; heart-healing

RUBY KYANITE Boosts cash flow and psychic awareness

RUTILE Brings manifestation, amplification of powers, and adaptation to energies

– S –

Crystal Facts: Sapphires

Sapphires, like rubies, are in the corundum family (see page 83). Blue sapphires are the most popular and well-known variety of this gem, but they come in a spectrum of colors.

Blue corundum is known simply as sapphire; corundum stones in other colors are called "pink sapphire," "yellow sapphire," and so on, or sometimes "fancy sapphires." The pink-orange padparadscha variety from Sri Lanka is the rarest sapphire; it can be more expensive than very fine blue stones. Madagascar is currently the world's largest producer of sapphires, while the most highly prized ones are from Kashmir, India.

Ancient Persians believed the Earth was balanced on a sapphire pedestal, which is what made the sky blue. Sapphires were used by Ancient Greeks to open the "third eye." Diana, Princess of Wales, had a 12-carat sapphire engagement ring, which Kate Middleton, Duchess of Cambridge, now wears.

SAPPHIRE

Blue Removes blocks and aids self-control, creativity, and wisdom

Padparadscha Improves passion, imagination, and spiritual visions

Pink Promotes kindness, love, and compassion

White Improves luck and good fortune; for insight, lucidity, awakening, and judgment

Yellow Can be used in rituals to help improve finances

SCAPOLITE Can be used in spellcraft to ease mental stress

SCOLECITE Most effective in communication rituals, especially when looking for a person of one's past

SCORIA (Lava rock) Dissipates angry emotions

SELENITE (Gypsum) For spiritual awakening, connection to the mystical, and angelic communication; creates a loving environment when placed in the home

Sunset gold Helps in understanding one's self and connecting to a higher power

SERAPHINITE (Clinochlore) Brings peace and contentment to life; also thought to promote wealth and prosperity (a very lucky crystal to own!)

SERPENTINE Used in spells to repair relationships

SHAMAN STONE Aids in spiritual awareness, shamanic journeying, energy cleansing, and balancing of chakras; can be carried as a protection talisman

SHATTUCKITE Encourages reception of information from one's spirit guide; a stone of truth, for use in spells to bring out truth

SHIVA LINGAM Thought to be mentally helpful in pregnancy and childbirth; sends positive energies

SHUNGITE A healing stone believed to help combat any health issue

SILLIMANITE For use in rituals to ward off rivals

SMITHSONITE Balances emotions, relieves stress, and boosts the immune system

SODALITE Removes sluggishness (good for motivating teenagers); for opening one's deepest thoughts and desires, perception, intellect, and prophetic vision

SPHALERITE Helps one draw strength from the earth; grounding; creates harmony

SPHENE (Titanite) Boosts intellect, perception, and wisdom

SPINEL Helps workaholics; releases any work-related fears or worries

SPODUMENE For use in rituals to stop obstacles relating to love

Triphane (yellow) Used to melt away negativity, leaving its user in a more positive frame of mind

STAUROLITE Sometimes known as the faerie stone; used for connecting with nature spirits, such as faeries or dryads; placing this stone beneath a tree encourages elemental energy

STIBNITE (Antimony sulfide) Helps when trying to adjust to changes in life; also helps stop pets from misbehaving

STICHTITE Helpful in any kind of ritual involving forgiveness

STILBITE Promotes spiritual harmony, clarity, insight, access to dream information, and lucid dreaming

STONEHENGE BLUESTONE Found at Stonehenge; helps connect its user to a higher spiritual consciousness; is thought to give access to the mystical, such as the spirit of Merlin and his magick

STROMBOLITE Brings fun and humor into life

STRONTIANITE For use in meditation, to bring about Kundalini awakening

SUGILITE Protects a person from catching the negative energy of others; good for counselors to carry or wear when supporting people who might be depressed; can be used to help a dying pet pass peacefully

SUNSTONE Brings light into the darkness of life; believed to attract financial abundance, positive energy, and guidance from spirits

—T—

TAAFFEITE Can inspire the mind and create original thinking

TANZANITE Often given to one's beloved in magickal communities; used in love magick to attract a soulmate; used as a healing stone

TEKTITE Thought to open one up to telepathic communication and a link with otherworldly energies and beings

> **Libyan gold** For protection against negativity, clarity of thought, and creativity; guards the aura

> **Tibetan** For opening chakras and cleansing; attracts light energy

THULITE Focuses on the Heart Chakra, happiness, harmony, compassion, kindness, and correction of negative energies

TIFFANY STONE (Purple passion) May give one's sex life a helping hand; helps its user grow psychically

Crystal Facts: Taaffeite

This sparkling gemstone was discovered rather recently, in the 1940s, by an Austrian Irish gemologist, Richard Taafe. He found it in a shop in Dublin, already cut and polished. It is sourced from Sri Lanka, Myanmar, and Tanzania, although very few specimens have been mined since its discovery, making it extremely rare. It is typically pink or lilac, but can also be colorless, green, blue, red, or bluish-violet.

TIGER'S EYE Protects one from the evil eye; releases fears and anxiety; helps families welcome new family members
> **Blue** Focuses on the Throat Chakra, communication, and expression
> **Red** May improve libido and promotes an active sex life

TIGER IRON (Mugglestone) Increases stamina and improves creativity

TOPAZ Has differing influences depending on the variety
> **Black** For healing, spiritual connection, and transcendental experience
> **Blue** Boosts psychic ability, spiritual growth, and spiritual communication
> **Golden** Improves generosity; is thought to bring riches
> **Silver** Used to lift negative energies; brings lasting stamina

TOURMALINE Offers protection during rituals; also attunes its energy to plants and acts as a natural insecticide; beneficial for use in the garden; can be used to boost business takings

> **Black** Gives protection from ill wishes; helps promote better sleep; used in spells to protect one's home from anything negative and to hopefully bring home lost pets
> **Blue** Helps melt away sadness; good for use in healing spells; is thought to help direct energy against infection
> **Brown** Stops dysfunctional family relationships; promotes creativity
> **Golden** Brings luck to business
> **Green** Gives strength to people overcoming addiction
> **Indicolite** Increases mental energy, so use in spells to combat fatigue
> **Paraíba** Helpful for calming down children
> **Pink** Produces harmony in relationship

Crystal Fact: Paraíba Tourmaline

The Paraíba tourmaline is an uncommon and beautiful bright blue-to-green stone prized for its rarity and incandescent glow, due to the presence of copper in the stone. Though discovered in and named for Paraíba, Brazil, the largest supply is found in the East African country of Mozambique. One carat of this stone will set you back approximately $16,000.

TREMOLITE A charm thought to encourage healing energy for heart conditions; offers access to mystical energies

TSAVORITE For finding inner beauty and possibly improving money situations

TUGTUPITE Considered the stone for unconditional love; helps balance intense emotions

TURQUOISE One of the most powerful stones for protection, especially during journeys; brings mystic awakening, spiritual communication, and union of the mind and spirit

– U –

ULEXITE Amplifies visualization and improves psychic abilities

UNAKITE Connects user with nature, including spirit animals and pets who have passed on

– V –

VANADINITE Believed to increase sexual prowess; removes creative blocks

VARISCITE Good to use in spells to stop sibling rivalry

VERDITE Helps one open the chakras and access spiritual knowledge; can induce kundalini awakening during meditation

VESUVIANITE Promotes inner security; is thought to release people from emotional imprisonment

VITALITE Helps remove anxiety and fear; helpful in public speaking

VIVIANITE Used by healers for absent healing

VORTEXITE Empowering, boosts inner strength

–W–

WAVELLITE Calms anger and aggression

WILLEMITE For transcendental communication and safe travel

WULFENITE Heals past-life relationships, leaving you free to love in the present

–Z–

ZEBRA STONE Believed to boost healing energy for bone- and heart-related issues

ZINCITE Promotes healing and taking action; promotes manifestation, resilience, and passion

ZIRCON Helps one understand feelings; gives one power needed for success

ZOISITE Thought to remove grief and control anger; healing when used in rituals if life has been traumatic; thought to help spells for conceiving a child

EASY REFERENCE GUIDE

When you have a spell in mind but aren't sure which stone to use, scan the following lists of stones grouped by purpose. If the name of a stone interests you, look up its entry in the A–Z list to make sure it corresponds to the task at hand. Remember, there are a variety of stones that can work for each category, so if you find it difficult to source one, you can always substitute another.

For Banishing Negativity

Ametrine · calcite (black [shamanite], blue, clear) · chalcanthite · chalcedony (blue) · chlorite · citrine · datolite · Eilat stone (King Solomon stone) · epidote · ironstone · jasper (black, kambaba [crocodile], leopard skin, ocean) · obsidian (black, snowflake) · opal (violet flame) · petalite · proustite · quartz (smoky, Tibetan black) · sillimanite · thulite · topaz (silver)

For Communication

Adamite · agate (blue lace, Ellensburg blue) · astrophyllite · · Eilat stone (King Solomon stone) · hemimorphite · kinoite larimar · opalite · scolecite · tiger's eye (blue)

For Confidence and Self-esteem

Agate (common, crab fire) · alexandrite · calcite (orange) · cassiterite · citrine · garnet (rhodolite) · goldstone · hematite · obsidian (mahogany) · opal (blue Peruvian) · plancheite · purpurite · quartz · (black phantom, eisen)

For Creativity

Agate (fire) · apatite (golden) · azurite · bustamite · calcite (orange) · goethite · goldstone · jasper (fancy, rathbunite) · kyanite (orange) · quartz (angel aura, green) · tiger iron · rhyolite (New Zealand/pakulite) · sapphire (blue) · vanadinite

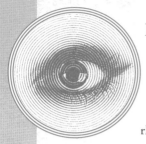

For Divination and Psychic Awareness

Albite • amblygonite • apatite (blue) • aragonite (blue)
• Azeztulite (red fire) • benitoite • beryl • cavansite •
chrysoberyl • covellite • halite (blue) • jeremejevite
• prophecy stone • quartz (tanzan aura, titanium) •
rhodizite • tektite • Tiffany stone • topaz (blue) • ulexite

For Emotional Matters

Agate (blue lace) • alexandrite • amethyst-cacoxenite • amber
• amblygonite • apophyllite (clear) • aquamarine • aventurine (blue) •
barite • beryl • brazilianite • calcite (clear, green, pink opaque) • cassiterite
• chalcedony (blue) • chalcopyrite • chrysoprase • charoite • cuprite
(crimson) • danburite • diamond • diaspore • Eilat stone (King Solomon
stone) • fuchsite • gaspéite • hackmanite • heulandite • hiddenite
• howlite • jade • jasper (kambaba, picture, spider) • jet • kunzite • lazulite
lepidolite (common, lilac) • malachite • Maori greenstone • morganite
• obsidian (snowflake) • opal (black precious) • papagoite • quartz
(anandalite, black phantom, blue, druzy, imperial gold,
witches finger) • scapolite • smithsonite • tourmaline
(blue) • variscite • vesuvianite • wavellite • zoisite

For Fertility and Family

Agate (blue lace, carnelian [banded]) • aventurine
• carnelian • fluorite • jade (jadeite and nephrite) •
obsidian (Apache tears) • rhodonite • quartz (rose)
• Shiva lingam • zoisite

For Happiness, Positivity, and Change

Adamite • aventurine • azumar • bastnäsite • beryllonite • bustamite • calcite (pink transparent) • chalcedony (blue, chrysoprase) • diopside (black star) • euclase • gaspéite • halite (pink) • heliodor • hemimorphite • jade (blue, green, purple) • jasper (mookaite, ocean, poppy, rathbunite) • odestone • magnesite • magnetite • merlinite (traditional, mystic) • moonstone (rainbow) • opal (Mexican fire, Oregon) • papagoite • piemontite • peridot • quartz (hollandite, pietersite, tangerine, titanium) • sapphire (white) • seraphinite • sphalerite • stibnite • strombolite • tourmaline (common, rubellite) • triphane • zircon

For Healing and Health

Agate (blue lace, crab fire, purple sage) • agnitite • amazonite • amethyst • ammolite • apatite (green) • aragonite (Spanish) • aventurine (green) • axinite • Azeztulite (amazez, black) • blizzard stone • bloodstone • cacoxenite • calcite (pink opaque) • carnelian • celestite (celestine) • cuprite • danburite • diaspore • gaspéite • goethite • greenstone • heulandite • jasper (brecciated, kambaba [crocodile], red) • larimar • lepidocrocite • lepidolite • moldavite • obsidian (black) • onyx • opal (common, white precious) • piemontite • quartz (angel aura, black phantom, clear, druzy, faden, harlequin, lithium, rainbow, Sichuan) • scapolite • shungite • tourmaline (green) • tremolite • vivianite • zebra stone • zincite • zoisite

For Houses and Homes

Andalusite ⁘ aragonite (star clusters) ⁘ bowenite ⁘ calcite (blue) ⁘ carnelian ⁘ celestite (celestine) ⁘ chalcanthite ⁘ citrine ⁘ datolite ⁘ hematite ⁘ jade (black) ⁘ jasper (black, spider) ⁘ quartz (clear) ⁘ selenite ⁘ tourmaline (black)

For Intellect and Learning

Calcite (honey, red) ⁘ chrysoberyl ⁘ quartz (harlequin) ⁘ hematite ⁘ herderite ⁘ lazurite ⁘ magnetite ⁘ muscovite ⁘ sphene (titanite)

For Legal Matters

Hematite ⁘ garnet (grossular)

For Love and Sex

Agate (fire) ⁘ ajoite ⁘ Azeztulite (pink, red) ⁘ bixbite ⁘ bloodstone ⁘ calcite (orange) ⁘ chrysocolla ⁘ creedite ⁘ darwinite ⁘ diopside ⁘ emerald ⁘ enhydro crystal ⁘ jade (green, nephrite) ⁘ jasper (fancy, red, unakite) ⁘ garnet (andradite, red, rhodolite, spessartine) ⁘ goethite ⁘ hiddenite ⁘ kinoite ⁘ kunzite ⁘ kyanite (orange) ⁘ opal (fire, Mexican fire, pink Peruvian) ⁘ moonstone ⁘ quartz (rose, ruby aura, Russian red, smoky, tangerine) ⁘ rhodocrosite ⁘ rhodonite ⁘ rhyolite (New Zealand/pakulite) ⁘ sapphire (padparadscha, pink) ⁘ serpentine ⁘ spodumene ⁘ tanzanite ⁘ Tiffany stone ⁘ tiger's eye (red) ⁘ tourmaline (pink) ⁘ tugtupite ⁘ vanadinite ⁘ wulfenite ⁘ zincite

For Luck, Success, and New Beginnings

Alexandrite · amber · aventurine (green) · Azeztulite · garnet (grossularite) · tourmaline (rubelite) · zircon

For Money and Work

Aventurine (green, red) · carnelian · chalcopyrite · chlorite · citrine · Gaia stone · garnet (green) · hiddenite · hypersthene · jade (green) · jasper (ocean) · jet · kyanite · malachite · opal (Mexican fire) · peridot · pyrite · ruby · sapphire (yellow) · seraphinite · spinel · sunstone · tiger's eye · topaz · golden · tourmaline (golden) · tsavorite

For Nature, Animals, and the Environment

Apophyllite (green) · chrysoprase · goethite · jasper (genesis, kambaba [crocodile], poppy, rainforest, unakite) · kyanite (green) · proustite · quartz (clear, Isis, Seriphos green, Siberian blue) · rhyolite · staurolite · stibnite · tourmaline

For Protection

Agate (common, crazy lace, eyes) · andalusite · Azeztulite · bowenite · bronzite · calcite (pink opaque) · chrysoberyl · diopside (chrome) · fluorite · garnet (almandine, black andradite) · hematite (rainbow) · jade (black, nephrite) · jasper (Dalmatian, leopard skin) · jet · labradorite · malachite · Maori greenstone · obsidian (black) · okenite · onyx · pyrite · quartz (witches finger) · shaman stone · sugilite · tektite (common, Libyan gold) · tiger's eye · turquoise · tourmaline (black) · willemite

For Sleep, Insomnia, and Nightmares

Angelite • amethyst • tourmaline (black) • quartz (clear, dream) • fluorite • garnet • lazulite • hematite • spessartine • jade • jasper (kambala [crocodile]) • labradorite • moonstone

For Spiritual Matters

Agate (purple sage) • ajoite • albite • amegreen • andesine • angelite • barite • beryllonite • bowenite • brookite • calcite (common, Merkabite, pink opaque, pink transparent) • catlinite • celestite (celestine) • danburite (agni gold) • fulgurite • Gaia stone • galaxite • galena • goshenite • hackmanite • hanksite • kinoite • kyanite (blue, indigo) • marcasite • moldavite • muscovite • obsidian (peacock) • okenite • opal (Oregon, Owyhee blue) • phenakite • prehnite • quartz (angel aura, cathedral [lightbrary], celestial [candle], clear, nirvana, prasiolite, spirit, titanium, white phantom) • selenite/gypsum (sunset gold) • shattuckite • stilbite • Stonehenge bluestone • strontianite • topaz (black, blue) • verdite

For Strength, Vigor, and Courage

Azeztulite (red fire) • bixbite • bloodstone • cuprite • garnet (almandine, green) • jasper • marcasite • obsidian (black) • quartz (molybdenite) • desert rose (crystal clusters of gypsum or barite) • sodalite • tiger iron • tourmaline (indicolite) • vortexite

Chapter 5

Everyday Crystal Spells

ONCE YOU BECOME A CRYSTAL ENTHUSIAST AND HAVE squirreled away a nice selection of stones, you can incorporate them into every single one of your spells. We have mentioned before that the size of the stone doesn't matter, and if you really want to keep the cost down, you can opt for smaller tumbled stones, which are easy to store and relatively inexpensive. Even small chips or slivers of crystal work well.

For best results, your stones should be cleansed and empowered (see pages 29–35) before a spell is performed to ensure that they are sterile and fully charged. If your spell uses a collection of the same stones or a variety of differing stones, don't worry; they don't need to be cleansed and charged individually. You can easily project your energy onto as many as twenty stones at a time, in the same way as if you were working with one.

BEFORE YOU
PERFORM A RITUAL

The following is relevant information and must be understood before
any ritual takes place.

Crystal Preparation

When empowering your stones or crystals, make sure that you
spend at least five minutes beforehand holding the stone and
envisaging the desired result of your spell in your mind's eye.
Because crystals absorb energies and emotions, the crystal
you plan to use will work better if it knows exactly what you
want it to do. If you have trouble visualizing, speak to your
stone out loud and express your wish to it.

Whatever your purpose, be assured that there *is* a crystal to
help. If the spells below call for a stone that you don't have, you can
always substitute a different one for it. Just refer to the easy reference
guide in chapter 4 (pages 91–96), which groups crystals by purpose and
situation, and pick a stone that sits in the same group.

The preparation and methods for the spells in this book will vary,
so be sure to read the entire spell thoroughly before commencing.
Follow each direction to the letter.

Candles

If your spell calls for the use of candles, then, unless otherwise stated,
these must be left to burn down on their own (always supervised, of
course). If you blow them out prematurely, your ritual may not be as

successful. Tealight or votive candles are well suited for this purpose. Please be vigilant when you light the candles and make sure that they are properly adhered to a suitable holder. Never leave a candle unattended or within reach of small children. Sometimes a spell will take place over the span of a couple of days. In these cases, the candle may be extinguished and relit later.

Closing the Ritual

Whenever you cast a spell, no matter its source, in many cases, it's a standard tradition that you repeat a chant or mantra. The number of times you recite the incantation varies from spell to spell, but it is essential that once you have spoken the ritual in full, you close it down by saying the words *"So mote it be."*

"Topping Up" Your Stone

When a crystal is present during a spell, it soaks in the ritual's aura and effects. If you use a crystal in a spell with long-term intentions, don't cleanse it after the spell. Instead, allow the crystal to radiate this power—it should last for at least two months. If the effects of your spell seem to begin waning after that time, and you need the spell to continue, the crystal may need to be "topped up." Go ahead and perform the spell a second time. Once a spell has worked and your final desired solution has been attained, then go ahead and cleanse your crystal.

General Crystal Intention Ritual

Before we get into the main part of this chapter, which lists spells by category (the categories are alphabetical—from spells to help children to psychic and spiritual spells), here is a general spell that can be performed for yourself or for a client. Merely hold the crystal you plan to use in your hand, focus on it, and speak directly to it, voicing your intentions.

For example, if you want a crystal to help bring you clarity, you might say: *"I ask that you help me see the truth in every situation."* If you are asking assistance for matters of the heart, say something like *"I ask that you send out your magick for all things romantic."*

When you've finished setting your intentions, give a little prayer of love, thanks, and gratitude to the universe and the crystals for their energy and their support of your plans.

SPELLS TO HELP CHILDREN

There is something about a child's innocence that helps crystals perform to the best of their abilities. This is probably why children are drawn to crystals like magnets. Kids have youthful energy that hasn't yet been contaminated by the outside world, so the stones can work their magick in a purer and more refined way.

A Spell for Protecting a Child

We all want to protect our children, from making sure that they are safe at school or while crossing streets, to keeping them safe from predators and unsavory people. This spell is versatile and encourages the guardians to shield your child, whatever their age.

Materials

> A tiger's eye stone
>
> A photograph of your child
>
> A lock of your child's hair
>
> A pillar or altar candle in white or preferably lavender scented, and a candleholder
>
> 1 tablespoon of dried angelica root
>
> A small drawstring pouch

Ritual

Cleanse and empower your tiger's eye (see chapter 2, pages 29–35). During a full moon phase, set up a small altar, placing your child's photograph in the center. Take the lock of hair and the stone and situate them directly in front of the photo.

Put the candle in a holder and situate it on top of the photograph before lighting it.

Angelica root summons the angels and has powerful protective properties. Sprinkle the dried angelica root around the photo, candle, stone, and lock of hair, forming a circle. Say the following spell once:

> *"Archangel Gabriel, custodian of children,*
> *please hear my plea this day,*
> *Shine down your powerful rays and blend your magick with mine.*
> *So mote it be."*

Then recite the following spell twelve times:

> *"Bring power to this magickal charm, let nothing*
> *appear to hinder or harm.*
> *Safely they stay in the arms of your love, the highest*
> *protection I seek from above."*

After you've recited the spell twelve times, close it by adding *"So mote it be."*
Let the candle burn for about an hour, then blow it out. Gather up the angelica
root, the stone, the photograph, and the lock of hair and place all the items inside
the drawstring bag. Hang this charm on the inside of your child's wardrobe or
closet and leave it there. Keep the candle somewhere safe. If your child ever goes
away or is outside of your care for any length of time, relight the candle. There is
no need to repeat the spell. Each time you light the candle, the magick will top up.

A Spell for Helping a Child Sleep at Night

We all know how important it is that children get their rest, but some kids
just don't sleep well. Others fear the dark and might cry and make a fuss,
and no matter how hard you try, nothing seems to work. Each night you
face this endless battle of wills. This spell will help quiet any child, from
a crying babe to a restless teenager. For this ritual we combine the powers
from two stones: amethyst and Columbian dream quartz. When united,
this pair creates the perfect energy in your child's bedroom, enabling them
to get a restful night's sleep.

Materials

An amethyst crystal

A Columbian dream quartz crystal

Paper and pen

A piece of string

A votive or tealight candle, in white

Meditative music

Ritual

This spell must be performed in your child's bedroom, during any moon phase. It is best done during the day while it is quiet. Cleanse and empower your crystals (see chapter 2, pages 29–35). Empower both stones at the same time and envisage your child sleeping soundly during the ritual. Write your child's name and the words *to be calm and settled* on the piece of paper. Make a small hole in the top of the paper and thread the string through it. Attach this written charm to the back of their bedroom door. Place the amethyst and dream quartz next to each other on a surface in the bedroom, such as a table, dresser top, or shelf, and light the candle.

Next play the meditative music while the candle burns (keeping close watch on it). When the flame has burned for about an hour, stand over the candle and say these words seven times:

"Darling child, your mood is sweet, calm and peaceful you shall be,
Gently will you drift to sleep, no more fears for you or me."

After you've recited the spell seven times, close it by adding *"So mote it be."* Let the candle burn down. When it has done so, place the stones somewhere in the child's bedroom where they will be out of reach. During the next few evenings as you are putting your child to bed, make sure you play the meditative music. You should see a difference straightaway.

A Spell to Guard Against Bullying

As parents, we can be extremely protective of our children, especially when they are bullied. If you decide to cast a spell to help stop bullying, it is essential that you be in the right frame of mind. Children who antagonize others are usually troubled in some way, so there's likely a reason for their misbehavior. A thought is a living thing, so if you are annoyed or enraged when you cast the spell, you are likely to send the bully the evil eye (see pages 176–77). The last thing you want is to unintentionally send harm to a child. True Wiccans never advocate this, so you must always be in control of your emotions. Black obsidian is the best crystal to spiritually discourage bullies. It may help protect your child without sending any negative vibrations to the perpetrator.

Materials

A black obsidian stone

A paring knife

A votive or tealight candle, in black, for banishing the bad

A votive or tealight candle, in white, for protection

Two candleholders

A photo of your child

A photo of the bully, if you can obtain one, although not required

A small plastic container with a lid

Spring water or rainwater, enough to fill the plastic container halfway

Paper and pen

A small white feather, to represent angelic vibrations

Ritual

This spell is so powerful that it will work during any moon phase. Cleanse and empower your obsidian (see chapter 2, pages 29–35). With the knife, inscribe the black candle with the bully's name and the words *banish with love*. Inscribe the white candle with your child's name and the words *surround with protection*. Place both the candles in suitable holders and situate them on your altar. Rest the photo(s) near the candles. Take the plastic container and pour the water into it until the container is about halfway filled. Write the bully's name on the paper and then write the words *banish the bully with love* seven times. On the paper's opposite side, write your child's name at the top and then the words *surround with protection* seven times. Fold the paper multiple times, until it fits inside the plastic container. Add the stone and feather to the water.

Make sure all the items are submerged in the water. Light the candles and say this spell seven times:

> *"Angels of light, I summon your protective power this day,*
> *Bless my child and keep them safe and free from intimidation,*
> *Bless all those who perpetrate and inflict pain.*
> *Shield them also in your divine light."*

After you've recited the spell seven times, close it by adding *"So mote it be."* Leave everything in situ on the altar until the candles have burned down. Remove the stone from the water and leave it outside to dry.

Place the lid on the plastic container and put it at the back of your freezer. This action will freeze the bullying and stop it in its tracks.

Make sure your child always keeps the stone nearby, especially while at school. It is now fully charged and will act as a protective talisman, keeping your child safe and out of harm's way.

A Spell for Helping Concentration

If your child has been daydreaming or procastinating instead of
doing their homework or preparing for upcoming exams, this
quick and easy spell will boost their concentration.

Materials

A honey calcite crystal

A handful of fresh rosemary, for concentration

Ritual

A waxing moon is the best time to cast this spell, as it holds power to remove
obstacles that stand in the way of progress. Cleanse and empower your crystal
(see chapter 2, pages 29–35). Set up your altar, then scatter some rosemary
on its surface. Rest your crystal on top of the rosemary. For parents who wish
to conduct this spell on their child's behalf, say this mantra thirteen times:

*"I summon the light, observant and bright, focused
and centered both day and night."*

Young adults who want to perform the spell for themselves should say the
following mantra thirteen times:

*"Exams will come, exams will go, I will thrive, this I know,
With crystal in hand, successful I stand."*

No matter which spell you opt for, after you've recited it the appropriate
number of times, close it by adding *"So mote it be."* Keep the crystal inside
the schoolbag and place the rosemary beside the study area at home. Young
adults should carry the stone in their pocket when taking any exams.

A Spell for Increased Patience

Let's face it: sometimes children can try the patience of any good parent. From time to time, our tempers fray and we end up losing control, shouting or saying something we later regret. If you want to control your emotions and be a calm and understanding parent, cast this spell with a small piece of blue lace agate.

Materials

> A blue lace agate stone
>
> A votive or tealight candle, in pale blue

Ritual

Cleanse and empower your agate (see chapter 2, pages 29–35). During any moon phase, light a pale-blue candle and place your stone next to it. Say the following spell thirteen times:

> *"When I need to shout and want to groan,*
> *I focus on my magickal stone,*
> *Kindly mind and a placid mood, with this spell*
> *I shall conclude."*

After you've recited the spell thirteen times, close it by adding *"So mote it be."* Allow the candle to burn down. It is a good idea to memorize this spell. Whenever you feel frustrated, walk out of the room, hold the agate, and repeat this mantra to yourself until you feel calm.

SPELLS FOR EMOTIONS
AND WELL-BEING

It's common knowledge in Wiccan circles that we shouldn't really cast spells when we are unhappy or unwell, but if you are feeling a bit low, need energizing, or are wanting to face your fears, crystals really can change the vibes that surround you, leaving you feeling more capable and mentally focused on going about your life.

A Spell for Beating the Blues

Just because it's spring doesn't mean we always have a spring in our step. Everyone gets a little blue from time to time or suffers over the smallest of things. Using ammolite in your spell will gently wipe away this angst, and its therapeutic properties will leave you feeling better in no time. Ammolite and all the noted ingredients, when used together, can help beat the blues.

Materials

A piece of ammolite

A votive or tealight candle, in white

A ginseng tea bag

2 teaspoons of dried basil

4 sage leaves

A small drawstring pouch

Cleanse and empower your ammolite (see chapter 2, pages 29–35). Set up an altar during any moon phase, placing the ammolite and everything except the ginseng tea bag on the altar's surface. Light the candle and focus on the flame for about three minutes. Imagine you are extremely happy and contented. While the candle is burning, make a cup of tea with the ginseng tea bag and sip it slowly. When the candle has burned down, collect the basil, sage leaves, and ammolite and pop them in the drawstring pouch. Leave the pouch under your bed. Your mood may lift within a few days, and any worries you have will not seem so important.

A Spell for Phobias

We all have fears. It's essential to have a photograph of your phobia or something to represent it. For example, if you have a fear of flying or of snakes, you could print out a picture of an airplane or snake from the internet. The trick with this spell is to use a combination of candle colors with a piece of blue chalcedony. This creates a calm ambience and gives off helpful energy.

Materials

A blue chalcedony stone

A picture that represents your fear

A votive or tealight candle, in white, for balance

A votive or tealight candle, in purple, to center yourself emotionally

A votive or tealight candle, in yellow, to calm nerves and fears

Ritual

Cleanse and empower your stone (see chapter 2, pages 29–35). During any moon phase, place the image of your phobia on the altar. Light all three of the candles next to the crystal on the altar and let them burn for an hour. When the hour is up, stand over the altar and say the following mantra three times while cupping the chalcedony in your hands:

"The time is right, the hour is here, to combat my horror and wipe out my fear,

No more terror, no more dread, my phobia is now dead."

After you've recited the spell three times, close it by adding *"So mote it be."* Allow the candles to burn down until they extinguish themselves; then rip up the picture into tiny pieces and throw it in the trash. Hold the stone each night for a week or two while you are relaxing. The power from the spell might need topping-up every six months or so.

A Spell for Calming Nerves

This antianxiety chant will help with any nervous behavior that might appear when you are out of your depth.

Materials

    A clear quartz crystal

    A vanilla-scented candle in a glass jar

Ritual

Cleanse and empower your crystal (see chapter 2, pages 29–35). During any moon phase, sit quietly, holding your crystal, with the candle burning in front of you. Close your eyes and focus on your breathing for about ten minutes or until you are in a relaxed frame of mind. Take the vanilla-scented candle in one hand and hold your crystal in the other.

Stand in front of a mirror and recite the following words twelve times:

"Lessen the pressure, let me be calm,
Force out the fear, keep Angels near,
So I am content, at any event."

After you've recited the spell twelve times, close it by adding *"So mote it be."* Allow the candle to burn for a couple hours, then blow it out. Relight it every day for a few hours until it has completely burned down. Whenever you think you might have a nervous attack, hold the crystal and recite the spell quietly to yourself.

A Spell for Improving Your Faults

It's safe to say that each of us has faults, and even if we try hard to correct them, from time to time they will rear their ugly heads. Before you can begin to correct a fault, you must own it, so be true to yourself. Only then will you be able to roll your sleeves up and try to combat it.

Materials

An axinite crystal

A votive or tealight candle, in purple

A handful of sea salt

Ritual

Cleanse and empower your crystal (see chapter 2, pages 29–35). During a new moon phase, make camp in your bedroom and safely light a purple candle somewhere in the room. Gaze at the flame for about five minutes and concentrate on your fault; then imagine yourself being free of it.

Run a warm bath and add a handful of sea salt and the crystal to the water. This will cleanse your stone and purify your body in preparation for the spell. (You can bring the candle into the bathroom with you so it is not left unattended.)

Soak in the tub for at least fifteen minutes. After your bath is done, return to your bedroom (bringing your candle back). Sit on the side of the bed and hold the axinite in your hands. Close your eyes. Try to clear your mind, concentrating once again on the fault that you want to be rid of. Visualize yourself surrounded in a purple light and then imagine that the light is magickally erasing that part of your character. You need to envisage the magick flowing upward through your body and out through the top of your head. Continue doing this for ten minutes before saying the following spell once:

"With water and salt I cure my fault;
with a candle flame I take the blame,
With the power from my stone I correct my sin;
this very night I shall begin."

After you've recited the spell, close it by adding *"So mote it be."* Let the candle burn until you are sleepy, then blow it out before you settle down for the night. Repeat this spell (including the bath) every night for a week, using the same candle and focusing on only one fault at a time. When you have conquered your imperfection, spend the next week concentrating on another character flaw. Conducting this spell will also enhance your spiritual side.

A Spell for Stopping Jealousy

If you are experiencing feelings of jealousy or bitterness, or if you are around someone showing signs of this, acquire green aventurine. It is particularly good for clearing away feelings of envy.

Materials

A green aventurine stone

2 cups of water, in a saucepan

2 teaspoons of white granulated sugar

A handful of fresh basil leaves

A spray bottle

Rituals

Cleanse and empower your stone (see chapter 2, pages 29–35). On a waxing moon, gently heat the water in the pan. When it begins to simmer, add the sugar and let it dissolve. Turn off the heat and add a small handful of fresh basil leaves to the water. Leave the mixture to cool for an hour. Once the liquid has cooled, place your crystal into the water. Leave it overnight. This steeping phase will result in a gem elixir, or crystal essence. The vibrational energy from the crystal and the basil leaves will spill out into the magickal water. The next morning, remove the basil leaves and the aventurine and transfer the potion into a spray bottle, shaking well to combine. If you are casting the spell on yourself, then every morning and night for a week, spray your hands and bare feet with the water. If you are performing the ritual for someone else, give them the stone as a gift.

A Spell for Fear of the Dark

Children can often have a fear of the dark, but there are also many adults who feel uncomfortable once the lights go out. Howlite is a beautiful crystal to sleep with and can eradicate any nighttime anxieties.

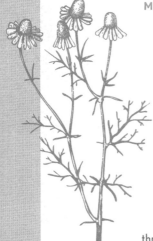

Materials

A howlite crystal or piece of howlite jewelery

A small bag of dried chamomile flowers, to cast out fear and leave you calm

A votive or tealight candle, in pale blue, and a candleholder

Ritual

Cleanse and empower your crystal (see chapter 2, pages 29–35). On an evening during any moon phase, place your howlite on your altar next to the chamomile flowers. Situate the pale-blue candle in a suitable holder and light it next to your items. Speak the following spell three times:

"With this crystal, I magickally charge, and no more will I fear the night,
My nervousness I now defeat, I sleep in slumber long and sweet."

After you've recited the spell three times, close it by adding *"So mote it be."* Hold your crystal about 6 inches (15 cm) above the flame of the candle for a few seconds and then leave it to burn down. You can scatter the chamomile around the base of your bed or put it into a pouch and tuck it inside your pillowcase. Keep the howlite on your nightstand. A good thing to do is to memorize the mantra and whisper it just before you sleep each night.

SPELLS FOR EMPLOYMENT AND WORK

On their own, crystals might not be able to win you a job or even improve your work environment, but when used in spellcraft, they can improve one's frame of mind when paired with the right job-searching tactics. Having a belief that the spells below will work can amplify the stone's ability.

A Spell for a Successful Interview

This spell, using the somewhat rare crystal hiddenite—a variety of spodumene that was originally discovered in North Carolina in the late nineteenth century—will give you the confident energy you need to ace your next interview.

Materials

A tiny piece of hiddenite

A pen, greeting card, and envelope

A votive or tealight candle, in green

A postage stamp

Ritual

Cleanse and empower your crystal (see chapter 2, pages 29–35). One week before your interview, purchase a greeting card and, on the inside, write your own name and the words *Congratulations on winning the job!* Place the tiny piece of empowered hiddenite crystal inside the envelope along with the card and seal it. Address the envelope to yourself. Place the sealed, addressed envelope on your altar; then light the candle beside it and say the following spell seven times:

"When the time to meet is finally here, they will hear me loud and clear.
With this spell I send a sign: I will succeed, the job is mine."

After you've recited the spell seven times, close it by adding *"So mote it be."* Allow the candle to burn down, then mail the envelope to yourself. Place the card on your mantelpiece or another prominent space in your home. Prepare for the interview thoughtfully, as you normally would, and hold the crystal in your hand or have it nearby (in your pocket, bag, or briefcase) throughout the interview.

A Spell for a Career Change

This is another spell involving the mailman and a piece of hiddenite. Writing yourself a letter often sweeps in good fortune, changing the energies around you from dull to exciting.

Materials

A tiny piece of hiddenite

A tall candle, in green, to summon a new job
and better prospects

Paper, pen, and envelope

A postage stamp

1 teaspoon of dried cinnamon

2 teaspoons dried basil

1 bay leaf

A long match or a long lighter

Ritual

Cleanse and empower your crystal (see chapter 2, pages 29–35). During any moon phase, light the candle on your altar. Take the paper and pen and start by writing down a list of all the kinds of jobs you might like to do, followed by this wording:

"Today, I am on a new journey.
Everything that is dull and boring in my life
will diminish and soon be replaced with an
exciting employment opportunity.
I have faith in myself and trust in the universe."

Fold up the letter and place it in the envelope. Sprinkle the cinnamon and basil into the envelope. Add the crystal and bay leaf. Seal it, affix the stamp, and address the envelope to yourself. Place the letter next to the candle and read the above words out loud. After you've recited the words, close the spell by adding *"So mote it be."* Allow the candle to burn until there is about one inch of wax left, then blow it out.

With a long lighter or match, carefully burn the base of the candle so that some of the wax drips onto the back of the envelope. Go straight out and mail the letter. While you wait for the letter's arrival, participate in standard job-hunting tactics. When the letter returns to you, open it and keep it somewhere safe. With patience and hard work, your fortune should soon change.

A Spell for Getting Promoted

Although green aventurine is traditionally used as a healing stone, it also carries unusual properties to help open doors in the business world. If you are tired of your job, want a promotion or merely seek to better yourself, this stone will unblock the career drains and give you a wealth of opportunities.

Materials

A green aventurine crystal

Your resume or curriculum vitae (CV)

A votive or tealight candle, in white

Ritual

The best phase for this spell is on the last day of a new moon, just before it begins to wax. This is a time when we can cast out a message for new beginnings and await the change. Cleanse and empower your crystal (see chapter 2, pages 29–35). Place a copy of your resume or CV on your altar. Place the crystal nearby and light the candle next to it. Say the following spell twelve times:

> *"Change afoot, a new job I'll find,*
> *my working life I leave behind,*
> *With good intent and crystal pure,*
> *new life, new job will come to the door."*

After you've recited the spell twelve times, close it by adding *"So mote it be."* Leave your resume or CV next to the candle while it burns down. Each time you apply for a new job or attend an interview, make sure that you either hold the crystal or have it on your person.

A Spell for Boosting a New Business

If you have just started a new business and want it to thrive, using tourmaline will prove effective. Remember, it can take time to get a business going, but with this spell, you should see things start to improve.

Materials

A tourmaline crystal

A small bowl

A packet of comfrey seeds, for business growth

10 drops of mandrake essential oil (a transporting oil)

A votive or tealight candle, in purple

A small gardening pot and soil

Water

Ritual

Spells for business work better if they are cast on a Thursday of a new moon phase. On this day, cleanse and empower your tourmaline (see chapter 2, pages 29–35) and place it in the center of the bowl. Empty the packet of comfrey seeds over the crystal and then sprinkle the contents with about ten drops of mandrake oil. Light the purple candle next to the bowl and say this spell nine times.

> *"My venture is alive and soon will start to grow,*
> *My business will thrive, with seeds that I will sow."*

After you've recited the spell nine times, close it by adding *"So mote it be."* While the candle is still burning, sprinkle a pinch of the seeds into the gardening pot and cover them with soil. Water it and leave on a windowsill. Take another pinch of the seeds and sprinkle them somewhere near the entrance to your workplace. As the seeds start to grow, so will the business.

A Spell for Helping a Business Thrive

Peridot crystals are wonderful for assisting with matters pertaining to the wealth and success of a business. Larger, faceted, gem-quality peridot crystals are not cheap, but don't worry; smaller pieces, like tumbled stones or chips, are just as effective. It's essential to perform this ritual on the business premises, so choose a place where you carry out most of your day-to-day tasks.

Materials

A peridot crystal

A purple drawstring bag

A votive or tealight candle, in purple

1 bay leaf

A black felt-tip marker

Ritual

Cleanse and empower your crystal (see chapter 2, pages 29–35). Do this on the first Thursday of a new moon phase. With the marker, write the name of your business along with the word *success* on the bay leaf.

Set up an altar and place the peridot on top of the bay leaf. Light the candle and say the following spell seven times:

"This crystal is alive; my business will forever thrive.
From above I am blessed, surround me now in your success."

After you've recited the spell seven times, close it by adding *"So mote it be."* When the candle has burned down, place the crystal and the bay leaf in the pouch and leave it somewhere safe on your business premises.

SPELLS FOR FAMILY-RELATED ISSUES

We all want the best for our family, and this selection of spells will hopefully help in the kind of situations that affect our loved ones the most.

A Spell for Improving Family Luck

As we have mentioned before, energy is infectious, so when someone in the family begins to experience a bout of bad luck, it can sometimes seep into every other member of the household. This spell will attempt to fill the family pot with success for everyone residing under the same roof.

Materials

> An amber tumbled stone for each member of the household
>
> Citronella oil
>
> A votive or tealight candle, in white, for each member of the household

Ritual

Cleanse and empower your amber stone(s) (see chapter 2, pages 29–35). On the morning of a new moon phase, collect your stones and dab each one with a little bit of citronella oil and place them on your altar in a line. Position the white candles behind each stone and light them.

Say the following spell as many times as there are stones (so if there are four people in the household, recite it four times):

> *"Ill fortune be gone; good luck has begun.*
> *I clear this space with magickal haste."*

After you've recited the spell the appropriate number of times, close it by adding *"So mote it be."* When the candles have burned, give each person a piece of amber and tell them to keep it close in the coming weeks. To provide the spell with extra clout, dab the front and back door with a little citronella oil. Luck should start to flow soon.

A Spell for Integrating New People into the Family

Getting the family dynamics right can often prove tricky. You might meet a new partner who could end up being a stepparent to your children, or one of the kids might find a new love interest, who could be then be spending more time in your home. Whatever your situation, using tiger's eye (to ward off negativity) and amethyst (to bring peace and happiness) to balance the energies will prove useful.

Materials

A tiger's eye stone

⅓ cup (50 g) of amethyst chips

A pretty bowl

0.35 ounces (10 g) of dried lavender, for tranquility

1 teaspoon of dried chives

A large candle, lavender-scented

A pen and small piece of paper

Ritual

Cleanse and empower your crystals (see chapter 2, pages 29–35). During any moon phase, take the pen and write the newcomer's name on the paper. Place the paper in the bowl, and then cover it with the amethyst chips. Rest the piece of tiger's eye on the top and transfer the dish and its contents to the altar. Sprinkle the dried lavender and chives over the top of the items, and light the candle beside it.

Say the following mantra three times:

> *"Welcome this newcomer into our lives, with crystal*
> *and lavender, amethyst and chives,*
> *Let us accept them with ease and with grace,*
> *a new family member we shall embrace."*

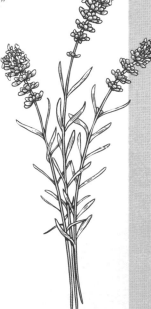

After you've recited the spell three times, close it by adding *"So mote it be."* After an hour, blow out the candle and leave everything on the altar undisturbed. For seven consecutive nights, light the candle again for one hour and recite the spell three times again, each time closing the session with *"So mote it be."* After the week has passed, move the bowl into the main living area of your home. If you chose to use a very large candle, you can relight it every now and again. This will top up the harmony.

A Spell for Stopping Warring Siblings

Battling siblings can be tiresome, especially when they are going at it all the time. You can magickally cement and soften their relationship by incorporating blue lace agate into this spell.

Materials

A blue lace agate stone for each sibling

A packet of powdered cloves, to stop arguments

A votive or tealight candle, in black

A votive or tealight candle, in white

Ritual

Cleanse and empower your stone(s) (see chapter 2, pages 29–35). While you empower them, take about twenty minutes to meditate on the bickering siblings and envisage them hugging or getting along well. On the night of a waning moon, place the agates into the package of powdered cloves and lay this on your altar. As you face the altar, situate the black candle to the left and the white candle to the right. Light the candles and say the following incantation nine times:

"Clashes and combat I will banish;
with this magick, the fighting will vanish.
I stop the quarrels, I join the ties;
no more lows, only highs."

After you've recited the spell nine times, close it by adding *"So mote it be."* When the candles have burned down, place one stone outside each of the siblings' bedroom doors and sprinkle a tiny amount of powered cloves around each one. The warring should stop within the week, and calmness shall reign.

A Spell for Sweetening the Mood of an In-law

If you have a critical mother-in-law (or any family member) who is always prickly and pointing their finger, you can cast a spell with the help of chrysocolla.

Materials

A rough chunk of chrysocolla

A bag of storebought potpourri

A pretty bowl

A small bag of dried lemon balm, for calm

A small bag of dried lavender, to bring peace

A votive or tealight candle, in pink, for love

A photograph of the family member

Ritual

Cleanse your crystal (see chapter 2, pages 29–35). On a waxing moon phase, empower your stone, focusing on the person in question and picturing them being nicer in general. Place the potpourri in the bowl and then mix in the dried lemon balm and lavender. Nestle the crystal somewhere in the bowl. Finally, rest the photograph on the top of the dish and light the candle nearby. Recite the following spell seven times:

> *"When they heckle, quiet their rage, reconcile us with this magick I've made.*
> *Every time they take a whiff, their behavior is sweet and their mood will lift."*

After you've recited the spell seven times, close it by adding *"So mote it be."* Allow the candle to burn down. The next time you visit the in-law or family member, give the bowl of potpourri as a gift. As the smell permeates their home, the magick will start to happen.

SPELLS FOR FERTILITY AND BIRTH

You may have noticed that there are fewer crystals listed in the A–Z Guide's "For Fertility and Family" category (chapter 4, page 92). After years of trying to help couples start a family and devising many spells and rituals to bring about this happy event, we have found that certain stones work exceptionally well. Creating another human being is a wondrous and complicated thing. Whether you're trying to bring a baby about naturally or through other means, timing is of the utmost importance.

A Spell for a Baby

Countless couples struggle for years to conceive a child. This is one time when you will need to handpick your stones very carefully. In the following spell, make sure that the maternal partner chooses the piece of rose quartz. Stinging nettle and patchouli oil, when paired with the power of rose quartz, unite beautifully to make a baby.

Materials

A piece of rose quartz

2 votive candles, in white

2 candleholders

Patchouli oil

A small bowl of dried stinging nettle leaves

Ritual

Set up your altar in advance and, aside from the items listed above, decorate it with anything that represents children in your eyes. You could opt for feathers, cherub figurines, baby booties, ribbons, pacifiers—the choice is yours.

On the first night of a full moon, play some peaceful music and cleanse and empower your rose quartz (see chapter 2, pages 29–35). Inscribe both candles with your full name, your partner's full name, and the words *Conceive a child.* Dip your finger into the patchouli oil and lightly smear the base of each candle. Place these in holders in the center of your altar. Rest the bowl of dried nettle leaves in front of the candles and, with your partner by your side, stand next to each other. The maternal partner must hold the quartz in their left hand, and the paternal figure must hold that same hand, so that the crystal is touching both partners. Light the candles and say the following spell once, in the order specified. Please feel free to modify this language so that it fits your particular situation.

> BOTH PARTNERS: *"Together we summon the universe, to grace us with a child that we can call our own. Allow us to be fertile together, united in our love. Give us this gift of life, no longer barren or unproductive."*
>
> PARTNER 1: *"Take my seed of life."*
>
> PARTNER 2: *"And let it grow within me."*
>
> BOTH PARTNERS: *"Give us our desire this day. We call upon the divine being to answer our plea."*

When you have finished reciting the spell, kiss your partner before the altar and close the spell by adding *"So mote it be."* One person should then take some of the dried nettle leaves and scatter them at the feet of the other. Place the crystal on top of the bowl of nettle leaves. When the candles have burned down and it's time for bed, take the bowl of leaves with the crystal and place it on the floor at the foot of the bed. Make love every night for a week while the moon is full.

Conception Spell #2

Babies can join families in all sorts of ways, so it makes sense to have another spell option. If the previous spell was not to your liking, give this one a go.

Materials

A jade stone

A small basket

A piece of baby-themed or white material, large enough to line the basket

1 free-range egg

A votive or tealight candle, in white

Patchouli oil

Ritual

A few days before the new moon, patch-test a few drops of patchouli oil on the skin of the more maternal partner, to test for allergies. Cleanse and empower your stone (see chapter 2, pages 29–35). Obtain a small basket (small enough to house an egg) and line it with a piece of baby-themed or white fabric.

On the first night of the new moon, place a fresh, free-range hen's egg in the basket and put it somewhere near your bed. Rest the jade next to the egg and light the candle. The paternal partner should dab a few drops of patchouli oil onto the lower abdomen of the maternal partner and rub it in in a circular motion while both parties make a silent wish for a child.

Make love while the candle is burning, and then straight afterward, cook the egg in whatever style you like and eat it together. Keep the jade under the mattress until you receive the news that a baby will join your family.

A Spell for Fear of Giving Birth

If you just found out you're pregnant and are terrified of giving birth, using Shiva lingam in this spell will provide you with the emotional strength you need to bring your baby into the world.

Materials

>A Shiva lingam stone
>
>2 votive or tealight candles, in yellow, for healing and health
>
>Vegetable oil

Ritual

Cleanse and empower your stone (see chapter 2, pages 29–35). One week before your due date, anoint the candles by smearing a little vegetable oil on the base of each one. Situate them on your altar, either side of the stone. Light the candles and say the following spell twelve times:

>*"I call upon my Mother Earth to ease the fear*
>*when I give birth,*
>*As I bring my infant to this life, there is no stress,*
>*there is no strife."*

After you have recited the spell twelve times, close by adding *"So mote it be."*

Let the candles burn down. When your labor begins, hold the stone or have it nearby; keep it close throughout the duration of your labor. You should feel calm and in control.

A Spell to Help with Labor

The presence of a crystal during birth can do wonders for a laboring mother's mind. Infusing black onyx with magick is thought to lessen the stress of childbirth.

Materials

> 2 black onyx stones
>
> A votive or tealight candle, in white

Ritual

A few days before the due date, the expectant mother must cleanse and empower the stones (see chapter 2, pages 29–35). During the empowering process, visualize the child being born with ease, with no complications or discomfort. Light the candle next to the stones and say this mantra twelve times.

> *"As I deliver my child to life, no pain,*
> *no stress, no pressure, no strife.*
> *I ask the goddess to hear my plea;*
> *make my labor trouble-free."*

After you've recited the spell twelve times, close it by adding *"So mote it be."* Allow the candle to burn down next to the stones.

When early labor starts, a family member must walk three times around the perimeter of the building where the mother is to give birth, holding one of the crystals in their left hand. The mother should have the other stone near the birthing bed. When the child is safely delivered, place both crystals at the bottom of the baby's crib. The magick from the spell will continue to influence the babe.

SPELLS FOR HEALING AND HEALTH

For centuries, people have used crystals and stones as healing implements. Although we cannot promise that a crystal will cure an illness or condition, they can be used to enhance one's psyche regarding medical conditions. Before we get into specific healing spells, we are including two rituals based on basic crystal grids or layouts; these can work well in conjunction with or in addition to the specific spells in this section. (Note: crystal grids will be covered in more detail in chapter 7.)

Creating a Crystal Circle

Choose stones that work best for healing (you can find a list on page 93). Many different types of stones can be used in this exercise, so you will need to stock up; but once you have around twenty different varieties of healing stones, you can create a *crystal circle*.

Clear a space in your living area and place all your stones in a large circle on the floor. To activate the crystals, you need to perform a deep meditation. You could ask a healer to sit inside the circle with you, in which case they will take you through the meditative process. (And if the person to be healed is someone else, they can sit in the circle too.) But if you are alone, make sure that you are sitting comfortably inside the circle and have no distractions.

Imagine that each stone is radiating purple and silver light, acting like a barrier around you, engulfing you in healing rays. Sit inside the ring for up to an hour at a time to receive the powerful healing properties of the stones. Please be aware that this exercise can sometimes leave you feeling a little light-headed. If you have this reaction, try lessening the amount of time you spend in the circle.

The Crystal Bed

A similar healing exercise can be done by using a bed. Place as many as twenty crystals all around your bed. Before going to sleep, practice the meditation previously described. Some people have custom-made crystals beds in their home. Some crystal beds look similar to a massage table, but the base is hollowed out and filled with seven containers of as many as fifty stones. This type of bed is so powerful that when you lie on it, you may feel as though the bed's energy is feeding directly into your seven chakras.

A Spell for General Healing

Most crystals have healing properties, but many are focused on specific ailments. Cuprite is an excellent overall healing crystal that can help with almost any illness. Witches also believe that the color yellow is all healing and so it is commonly used in crystal craft for its health-giving energy.

Materials

A cuprite crystal

Seven votive or tealight candles, in yellow, for healing

Cleanse and empower your crystal (see chapter 2, pages 29–35). During any moon phase, set up an altar, placing the crystal in the center. Position the seven yellow candles around the outside of the crystal and light them. Say the following spell seven times:

> *"Ailments will vanish, in good health I'll be,*
> *Banish my illness, let me be free."*

If you are performing the ritual for someone else, place a photograph of the person next to the crystal on your altar and change the wording to the following, being sure to recite it seven times:.

> *"Ailments will vanish, in good health they'll be,*
> *Banish this illness, let them be free."*

After you've recited the spell of your choosing seven times, close it by adding *"So mote it be."* Everything on the altar must remain untouched until the candles have burned down. The person who is sick must keep the crystal in the living room of their home and carry it when out and about.

A Spell for a Better Night's Sleep

We all know that, to function properly, we need sleep, but if you find it hard to doze off at night or have periodic bouts of insomnia, you might want to make an amethyst sleep pouch.

Materials

An amethyst crystal or a few amethyst tumbled stones

2 teaspoons of anise seeds

3 teaspoons of dried peppermint leaves

A bowl or dish

1 bay leaf

1 cedar incense stick

A small, purple drawstring pouch (purple is the color for inducing sleep)

Ritual

Cleanse and empower your crystal(s) (see chapter 2, pages 29–35). On the evening of a waxing moon, go into your bedroom and begin the spell by mixing the anise seeds and dried peppermint leaves in a bowl. Place the bay leaf and the amethyst(s) on top of the mixture. Light the cedar incense stick next to the bowl and let it burn down. All these items are magickally renowned for inducing sleep. When this is complete, take the cooled ashes from the incense and mix them in the dish with the other ingredients. Transfer the herbs, ashes, and crystal into the drawstring pouch and then place it inside your pillowcase. As you get into bed each night, recite the following spell:

"Sleepy slumber, tranquil rest,
I am peaceful, I am blessed,
Beneath my head tonight I keep
The magickal items to aid my sleep."

Each time you recite the spell, close it by adding *"So mote it be."*
You'll be snoozing like a baby in no time!

A Spell for Feeling Energized

Most of us lead hectic lives and are often overworked; this can leave us feeling sluggish and lethargic. Bloodstone possesses magickal properties that boost energy and leave us feeling invigorated.

Materials

A polished bloodstone

An oak leaf, for strength

A votive or tealight candle, in red

Ritual

Cleanse and empower your stone (see chapter 2, pages 29–35). Venture outdoors during any moon phase and find an oak tree. Hold your bloodstone against the bark of the tree and ask it to help you feel more energized and motivated. Take one leaf from the tree, being sure to thank it. Back at home, set up an altar. Place your stone on top of the leaf and light the candle. Say the following mantra twelve times:

> *"Energy and drive will be my prize,*
> *My body, my soul, I sanitize."*

After you've recited the spell twelve times, close it by adding *"So mote it be."* Leave everything in situ on the altar until the candle has burned down. Place the leaf inside your shoe for at least a week and sleep with the stone nearby at night.

A Spell for After Surgery

If you are unfortunate enough to need surgery, this spell may be useful to you. Along with following your doctor's post-surgery care instructions, this spell will work to help you feel more stable after your operation.

Materials

A small green aventurine tumbled stone, to promote healing

A small bowl of natural sea salt, for protection

A votive or tealight candle, in yellow or gold, for good health

Arnica essential oil, to promote healing

Ritual

Cleanse and empower your crystal (see chapter 2, pages 29–35). A few days before your surgery, set up your altar and rest the bowl of salt in the center. Completely bury your crystal in the salt so that you can't visibly see it. Anoint the candle by dipping your finger into the arnica oil and smearing it around the base of the candle. Leave the oil on the altar with the lid off. Light the candle and say the following spell twelve times:

> *"I summon a shield from the goddess above, to grace*
> *me in health and shower me in love,*
>
> *As my operation nears, I will bask in your light,*
> *a quick recovery, the future is bright."*

After you've recited the spell twelve times, close it by adding *"So mote it be."* Let the candle burn down, then remove the crystal from the salt and dab it a few times with the arnica oil. Make sure you take the stone into the hospital with you when you have your surgery. Leaving it in a bag beside the hospital bed is fine. When you return home, every day, pat a little arnica oil into each side of your neck.

A Spell for Magickally Alleviating Allergies

Wiccans believe it is possible to magickally rid yourself of any minor allergy, be it to animals, dust, hay fever, or scented sprays. The following is an old wives' tale, updated and transformed into a spell to help you ward off the sniffles.

Materials

> An agnitite crystal
>
> 1 large potato
>
> An apple corer
>
> A pen and piece of paper
>
> String
>
> A votive or tealight candle, in white
>
> Optional: a gardening pot, filled with soil

RITUAL

Cleanse and empower your crystal (see chapter 2, pages 29–35). In the morning of the first new moon in the month, take the agnitite into the kitchen and place it on the counter. Cut the potato in half and, with an apple corer, carve out a thick circle in each half of the potato, being sure not to puncture all the way through. Write down your name on a small piece of paper and list the allergy that you want to be rid of. For example:

> *"Leanna Greenaway*
> *To be free of my allergy to cats."*

Roll the small piece of paper into a tube and slot it into the holes of the potato. Put the two halves of the potato back together and secure it with string. Light the candle next to the potato and stone and say the following spell once:

"Reactions gone, allergy free; no more shall I suffer, so mote it be."

When the candle has burned down, bury the potato outside in the soil, or you can use a gardening pot. As you cover the potato with the last shovel of dirt, repeat the mantra again. Keep the crystal nearby during the times when your allergy is usually worse. You can perform this spell every time the symptoms return.

A Spell for Easing Fatigue

As we get older, it is not uncommon for us to feel more tired than usual. Indicolite harnesses power to help prevent this, leaving us feeling more energetic and animated.

Materials

An indicolite crystal

4 ounces (113 g) of baby talc (or any gentle base powder)

2 teaspoons of ginseng powder, to boost energy

A votive or tealight candle, in red, for vigor

Ritual

Cleanse and empower your crystal (see chapter 2, pages 29–35). When the moon is waxing, mix the talc and ginseng in a bowl. Blend it for a few minutes with the tips of your fingers (as though making pastry). Rest the crystal on top of the powder and transfer it to your altar. Light the candle beside the dish and say the following chant three times:

"With magickal items before me, improve my vigor and energy,
My mind is alert and my body is strong, all lethargy is now gone."

After you've recited the spell three times, close it by adding *"So mote it be."*

Allow the candle to burn down and then take the powder and scatter a small amount around the base of your bed. Every time you vacuum, be sure to replace the powder with some more. If you are feeling tired, hold the crystal for a few minutes to receive a flash of energy.

SPELLS FOR HOUSE AND HOME

The walls of buildings and homes absorb energy like a sponge. From the very first moment a place is built and occupied, every conversation, happy occasion, or full-on fight is recorded within its walls. Therefore, the more sensitive among us can walk into a building, old or new, and either get an eerie, shivery feeling or experience a lovely, positive vibe. When you first move into your house, regardless of whether your home is old or new, you must cleanse it of any energy left behind.

Using sage smudging sticks is probably the most effective way to do a spiritual cleaning. Holding the smoking bundle of sage in one hand (please exercise caution while lighting the sage), use your other hand to waft the smoke through the room. Repeat this simple ritual in every room and each nook and cranny in the house. If you want, you can even smudge the outside. Once you have done this preliminary procedure, you can go ahead and cast spells to safeguard the property for the future.

A Spell for Protecting the Home

Black tourmaline is, without a doubt, the best crystal to use for keeping your home safe and protected from negative emotions. You will need to acquire multiple pieces of black tourmaline—one tumbled stone for every main room in the house. So if you have a living room, dining room, and kitchen along with two or three bedrooms, it is essential that you have a stone for each room. Don't worry too much about cubbyholes or under-stair cupboards; this ritual is just meant for the places you use on a daily basis.

Materials

Black tourmaline, one piece for each room of your home

2 votive or tealight candles, in white

1 ¼ cups (300 ml) water

A bowl, large enough to hold the water

7 drops of witch hazel, for protection

A spray bottle

Ritual

Cleanse and empower your crystals (see chapter 2, pages 29–35). During any moon phase, light two white candles before pouring the water into the bowl. Add seven drops of witch hazel and then carefully submerge each piece of tourmaline in the water.

Say the following incantation seven times:

"With these pieces of tourmaline, let them act as a protective screen,
Blanket this home with blessings bestowed, shield this space, guard this abode."

After you've recited the spell seven times, close it by adding *"So mote it be."*

Allow the candles to burn down for an hour, leaving the tourmaline submerged in the water. After the hour has passed, blow out the candles; remove the stones from the bowl and let them dry. Transfer the water from the bowl into the spray bottle and twist the nozzle so that it is set to spray a fine mist. Go into each room of the house and place one stone somewhere near the window or door. Before you leave each room, spray the water high into the air a few times so that the mist falls gently into the room.

You might find that you have some protective water left over. It's a good idea to save this so you can squirt a few drops into the room next time you do a thorough cleaning.

Repeat this spell three or four times per year to keep the energies pure. You can also perform the ritual again if tensions are running high with members of the house or if someone has been unwell.

A Spell for Blessing a Home

There are many ways to bless a home, but none is better than twinning hematite with clear quartz. Together these crystals create harmonious energy, leaving the house free of all things negative.

Materials

> A hematite stone
>
> A clear quartz crystal
>
> 7 votive or tealight candles, one each in blue, pink, yellow, white, green, purple, and red, and 7 candleholders
>
> Sage incense, one stick for each room in the house

Ritual

Cleanse and empower your crystals (see chapter 2, pages 29–35). During any moon phase, place all seven candles in suitable holders and set them in a circle in the center of your altar before lighting them. Lay the crystals in the center of the candle ring, and put the unlit incense sticks around the outside of the candle ring.

Say the following mantra seven times:

> *"I bless this home with all that is pure;*
> *joyous light resides in the walls.*
> *Positive energy from ceiling to floor,*
> *in every room and every door."*

After you've recited the spell seven times, close it by adding *"So mote it be."* Allow the candles to burn for about thirty minutes. During this time, light one incense stick in every room of the house. You can bypass cubbyholes or under-stair cupboards. Allow the candles to burn down completely. Place the crystals on a sideboard or table in the main living area of your house.

A Spell for Stopping Difficult Neighbors

There are so many people the world over who are fed up because they live next door to someone who is making their life a misery—there's nothing worse! Whether they be nosy, noisy, or argumentative, you can attempt to put a stop to the disruption once and for all. Datolite of any variety is the perfect stone to use. It radiates calming energy that will change the mood of even the most difficult people.

Materials

A datolite crystal

A framed picture of an angel or goddess

A large altar or pillar candle, lavender-scented

Ritual

Cleanse and empower your crystal (see chapter 2, pages 29–35). This spell works best with deep visualization and can be done during any moon phase. While empowering your stone, imagine the people living next door to you being kind and polite; they are the perfect neighbors. Visualize them, being distracted from you and pursuing other interests. Continue with this meditation for a few minutes.

For the best results, take the framed picture of the angel or goddess and hang it on a wall in your home so that it is facing your neighbor's property. If you live in an apartment and your neighbor is above or below you, hang it somewhere in the center of your home. Set a small table underneath the picture and rest the candle there. Place the crystal on the floor directly underneath the table. Light the candle and say the following spell twelve times:

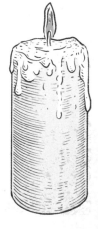

"Hear me, angel/goddess, hear my calls,
bless those who dwell outside these walls,
Quiet their lifestyle, soothe their space,
so we live in peace, each in our place."

After you've recited the spell twelve times, close it by adding *"So mote it be."* Let the candle burn for a few hours, then relight it every evening (extinguishing it before going to bed, for safety) until it has burned out completely. You can repeat this spell as often as you like to ensure that you live in peace.

A Spell for Moving to a New House

If you own or rent, this spell will unblock any clogged energy that might have previously stopped you from moving. Always perform house-moving rituals on Tuesday evenings, and use pale-blue candles; they tend to be more effective.

Materials

> An Azeztulite crystal
>
> A citrine crystal
>
> A votive or tealight candle, in pale blue
>
> A handful of acorns, for a fresh start
>
> Optional: a wand, any type

Ritual

Cleanse and empower your crystals (see chapter 2, pages 29–35). On a Tuesday of a new moon phase (the moon should be visible), place your candle, acorns, and crystals on the altar. Safely light the candle, and then go outside. Hold your wand in your left hand (if you do not own a wand, use your pointer finger). Raise both arms in the direction of the moon and say this spell three times.

> *"I call upon the moon this day to clear the obstacles quickly away,*
> *With speed and swiftness, I shall flit,*
> *my life will improve the moment I move."*

After you've recited the spell three times, close it by adding *"So mote it be."* Leave everything on the altar, including the wand, until the candle has burned down. Take the crystals and the acorns and bury them in your garden. If you don't have a garden or access to local woods, bury them in a pot of soil and leave it outside or by your front door.

A Spell for Getting a Mortgage Approved

It's nail-biting, waiting for a loan or mortgage to be approved, but you can try to ensure its success by inviting sunstone into your life. For best results, this spell should be cast on a Wednesday of a new moon phase.

Materials

A stick of cinnamon

10 cloves

A small bowl or container with a lid

1 cup of vegetable oil

A sunstone

NOTE: Don't throw away your oil; instead transfer it to a sealable container. This will work as an anointing oil for any money rituals you might want to perform in the future.

Ritual

Before you begin, you will need to make Money Oil. To do this, place the cinnamon stick and cloves in a small bowl or container and pour the oil on top. Cover the bowl or put the lid on the container. It is important to leave this to infuse at least overnight, so make sure you do this well in advance.

The next Wednesday evening of a new moon, cleanse and empower your crystal (see chapter 2, pages 29–35). Place your crystal in the bowl with the Money Oil so that the oil entirely covers it. Situate this on your altar. Say the following spell seven times:

> *"With obstacles removed, my loan is approved,*
> *cash is in sight on this new moon night."*

After you've recited the spell seven times, close it by adding *"So mote it be."* Remove the stone from the bowl of oil and dry it. This crystal is now energized and should be placed on a windowsill to attract the money you need.

A Spell for Clearing a Haunting

Ghosts are the usually harmless spirits of people who once walked the earth. A ghost is a soul who, for whatever reason, failed to go to the light at the point of death and chose to remain in situ. Some spirits can be oblivious to us and do not even realize that they are dead, whereas others can be noisy and more disruptive. If you live in a haunted house, this spell will hopefully help the spirit cross over to the other side.

Materials

A black jade stone

A bowl of salt

A sage smudging stick

A large white feather

Ritual

Cleanse and empower your stone (see chapter 2, pages 29–35). (Note: This spell can be cast at any time, although waxing moons can give the spell more clout.) When you empower your black jade, make sure that you visualize the trapped spirit transporting upward in a beam of golden light. Continue with this positive thinking for around ten minutes and then place your crystal and the salt on the altar. Ensure that all windows and doors in the home are closed. To remove any negative energy, you will need to light the sage smudging stick and, when you can see the embers, gently blow it out. (Please exercise caution while lighting the sage.) Once the sage is smoking, hold it in your left hand and the feather in your right. With the feather, repeatedly waft the smoke over the altar.

Retrieve the bowl of salt, but leave the crystal where it is. Go into every room and nook, even the small cupboards, and waft the smoke as before, but this time into the air. Recite the following spell once in each room of the house, making sure you are fearless and powerful. Remember: you are instructing the spirit to leave, so don't be bashful.

"I order the spirit of this house
to leave and go up to the light,
I command you to go through the door;
you are not welcome anymore.
Vacate this space and leave with love;
take flight and transcend up above."

After you've recited the spell in each room of your home, close it by adding *"So mote it be."* When you have done this, throw a handful of salt on the floor of each room and open a window so that the spirit can leave. When this part of the spell is complete, return any remaining salt to the altar and place the crystal on top. Extinguish the sage. After an hour, you can close all the windows. Leave the jade and salt on the altar for a week. You should start to feel the energy in the home become lighter.

A Spell for Ridding Your Home of Spiders and Insects

Spiders are attracted to witches and usually make a beeline straight for them, or their houses. You should never kill a spider intentionally, as it is bad luck. Instead, you need a good spell, like this one, to gently rid your home of spiders—and any insects—by inviting them to leave.

Materials

A spider jasper stone

A spray bottle

Spring water or rainwater

5 drops of citronella oil

5 drops of peppermint oil

5 drops of tea tree oil

A cobweb

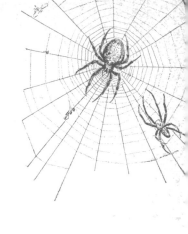

Ritual

On any moon phase, cleanse and empower your spider jasper stone (see chapter 2, pages 29–35). While empowering your stone, visualize all kind of insects, big and small, exiting your home through the doors and windows. Next, venture into the kitchen to prepare your potion. Half fill the spray bottle with water. Add each of the oils. Lightly roll the cobweb small enough so that it can be pushed inside the bottle. Screw the lid on tight and shake the bottle before placing it on your altar. Light one of the candles next to the bottle. Repeat the following spell three times, specifying your troublesome insect:

"{INSECT} receive me,
listen well: in my home you do not dwell,
Find a place away from here,
with love and light you must disappear!"

After you've recited the spell three times, close it by adding *"So mote it be."* Place the stone on the floor beside the home's main entrance. Spray all the skirting boards and door frames in your home with the magickal water. You can also squirt the potion under the beds. To stop insects from landing on you, you can even spray yourself. Continue to burn lavender-scented candles in the evenings for at least a week. The little darlings should hopefully move out.

SPELLS FOR LOVE AND ROMANCE

Whether you are in a relationship you want to improve or are single and looking for someone special, crystals are thought to magickally bring about and safeguard love.

Candles are a must with any love spell, and pink and red are always the preferred colors. Make sure you purchase tealight or votive candles as opposed to larger tapered candles or chub-like ones. Votive or tealight candles are much smaller and burn down in just a few hours, and since most love spells should be cast in the evenings, the last thing you need is to sit awake, waiting for the candle to extinguish itself, or fall asleep before it's done burning.

The best time to cast any spells pertaining to love is during a full moon phase, and Fridays are the favorite day.

A Spell for Finding True Love

If you are single and looking for a new love affair, the properties in kunzite might attract romance to your life.

Materials

A piece of kunzite, at least 1¼ inch (3 cm) in circumference

A votive or tealight candle, in pink

Patchouli oil

1 foot (30 cm) piece of thin ribbon, in red or pink

Cleanse and empower your crystal (see chapter 2, pages 29–35). On a Friday evening of a full moon phase, set up your altar and lay out your items on its surface. Light the pink candle. Add a few drops of patchouli oil to the kunzite. Repeat this spell twelve times:

"Magickal blessings bestow,
from this day on love will grow,
I cast out a message that shall be received;
entice my love here to me."

After you've recited the spell twelve times, close it by adding *"So mote it be."* Allow the candle to burn down. When it has extinguished itself, take the ribbon and wrap the crystal until there is just enough ribbon left to tie a bow.

Keep the stone nearby at all times—in a pocket, wallet, purse, or backpack. As a final suggestion to help love along, make sure that you accept social invitations and don't just stay at home behind closed doors.

A Spell for Attracting a Companion

Not everyone wants romance, passion, and excitement; some simply crave company and companionship. If you want to attract a friend to spend time with or just someone to go out and about with, use moonstone. It is the perfect crystal to bring this kind of friendship into your life.

Materials

A small tumbled moonstone or moonstone jewelry

A piece of paper and pen

A bowl

½ cup (24 g) of dried lovage

A votive or tealight candle, in pink

Ritual

Cleanse and empower your moonstone (see chapter 2, pages 29–35). On a Friday night of a full moon phase, write the words *To find a nice companion* on the paper seven times. Fold the paper once or twice so that it fits in the bowl, then pour the dried lovage on top. Situate your moonstone on top of the lovage and light the candle.

Recite this spell seven times.

> *"I seek ahead; I seek behind,*
> *an excellent companion I shall find,*
> *This stone is charmed with magick pure,*
> *to attract a friendship to my door."*

After you've recited the spell seven times, close it by adding *"So mote it be."* Allow the candle to burn down. The next morning, take the bowl and its contents outside. Scatter some (but not all) of the herb into the air. Bring the dish, complete with moonstone, back into the house. Leave it near the front door for at least two weeks. For those of you who prefer jewelery, after the two weeks is up, wear the moonstone every day for a further two weeks. If you opted for a tumbled stone, carry it with you in a pocket for the next two weeks. Help the spell along by joining a new group or a club; as with all love spells, don't lock yourself away.

A Spell to Stop Bickering and Create Harmony in a Relationship

Even the best relationships undergo difficulties that cause a couple to lose the connection that brought them together in the first place. This spell calls for the use of smoky quartz, which is lovely for calming emotions and stopping arguments that may arise.

Materials

- 2 smoky quartz crystals
- 2 votive or tealight candles, in pink
- 1 cup (50 g) of dried lavender
- A bowl
- 2 pieces of cloth, in pink, enough to completely cover each crystal twice
- A needle and thread, in pink

Ritual

Cleanse and empower your crystals (see chapter 2, pages 29–35). On a new moon phase, set up your altar and light the candles. Put the dried lavender in the bowl and place the crystals on top. Repeat the following spell three times:

> *"Arguments cease, this feud will decrease.*
> *Unite our love, and we shall have peace."*

After you've recited the spell three times, close it by adding *"So mote it be."* While the candles burn, lay out your two pieces of material and sprinkle approximately half of the dried lavender in its center. Take one of the crystals and rest it on top of one of the fabric pieces. Fold the cloth over the crystal until it is completely covered and then stitch it closed using the pink thread. You should end up with half of the lavender and one of the quartz pieces inside the fabric pouch. Repeat this with the other crystal. Leave both pouches on the altar and allow the candles to burn down.

Once the candles have extinguished themselves, place the pouches in the bedroom where you and your partner sleep. One pouch should be near your side of the bed, and the other should be near your partner's side. If your partner doesn't live with you, give them the pouch as a lucky charm and tell them to keep it in their bedroom. The magick will happen while you both sleep.

A Spell for Spicing Up Passion

It's very common for relationships to go through a dry spell from time to time, especially if you've been with the same person for years. If lust has left your relationship, fear not—this spell may help reignite your spark. You will need access to a bathtub for this spell.

Materials

A fire agate stone

A votive or tealight candle, in red, for passion

2 empty oyster shells, for all things sexual

Ritual

Cleanse and empower your stone (see chapter 2, pages 29–35). On a waxing moon phase, run yourself a bath with your choice of bath products. Submerge your crystal in the tub. Place the red candle somewhere in the bathroom and light it. Enter the bath. After a few minutes of relaxation, take the oyster shells and fill them with the bath water. Hold one in each hand and recite the following spell three times:

"Passion is mine, my sex life divine,
with crystal and shell, all will be well."

After you've recited the spell three times, close it by adding *"So mote it be."* Spend the remainder of your time in the tub relaxing and bathing. When you have finished your bath and exited the tub, retrieve the shells, the lit candle, and the crystals and place them beside your bed. Do not blow the candle out; instead, allow it to burn down on its own.

If you like, treat yourself to some lingerie that makes you feel sexy, confident, and empowered. You and your partner can enjoy it together.

A Spell for Forgiving an Unfaithful Lover

After an affair, whether you decide to leave the relationship or stay and face the music, this spell may help you heal a broken heart and see things more rationally. This spell employs dried hawthorn leaves (a tonic for the broken heart), a white rose (for matters relating to the heart), and fresh rosemary (to aid forgiveness).

Materials

A green calcite crystal

One votive or tealight candle, in pink, for love

3 teaspoons of dried hawthorn leaves

A sprig of fresh rosemary

The petals from a single white rose

A small drawstring bag

Ritual

Cleanse and empower your crystal (see chapter 2, pages 29–35). On a waning moon phase, light a pink candle and set it on your altar. Place your crystal next to it. Scatter the dried hawthorn all around the worktop. Pull the leaves off the sprig of rosemary. Sprinkle them over the top of the green calcite. Recite the following incantations seven times while placing one rose petal at a time on the altar:

> *"With these petals I now place,*
> *forgiveness will engulf this space,*
> *I evoke the magick from this spellcast; no more*
> *will I dwell on times that have past."*

After you've recited the spell seven times, close it by adding *"So mote it be."* Let the candle burn all the way down and then gather the hawthorn, rosemary, rose petals, and crystal. Place them in the drawstring bag and tie it closed. Place this pouch under your mattress. Within a few weeks, you should start to feel better.

A Spell for Moving On after Love

No matter the form of separation, it can be painful to move on when a relationship has ended. This spell will give you a sense of calm realization that will help you put the past behind you. Rhodochrosite is the perfect crystal to help with this, as it balances the Heart Chakra and promotes self-forgiveness. It can even bring new love into your life!

Materials

A rhodochrosite crystal or tumbled stone

A votive or tealight candle, in white

Ritual

Cleanse and empower your crystal (see chapter 2, pages 29–35). On the first night of a new moon, go to your bedroom, place the candle on your nightstand, and light it. Turn down the lights and sit on the side of your bed. Study the flickering flame for a few minutes. Cast your mind back to a time before your relationship, a time when you were happy and content. Embrace this feeling and think about how you want to feel in the future. After about five minutes, lie on your bed and rest the crystal over your heart, placing your hand over the top to keep it from moving. Say this mantra twelve times.

"Heal my heart, heal my soul, forever happy is my goal."

After you've recited the spell twelve times, close it by adding *"So mote it be."* After about thirty minutes, blow out the candle. Leave the rhodochrosite next to the bed. Repeat this spell every night until the moon begins to wax.

SPELLS FOR MONEY

There has always been some controversy within Wiccan circles as to whether it's ethical to summon magickal cash. What many people don't realize is that there is a universal pot of money that we can draw upon when we need a helping hand financially. Often, when you perform spells for cash, you will receive only what you need. The cosmos has a strange way of knowing just exactly how much is required, so rest assured, it is perfectly acceptable to perform magick to boost your cash flow.

Many crystals attract wealth and prosperity, so it's useful for a witch to have at least one money luck stone nestled in among your collection. It is also important to note that for a money spell to work successfully, it is best to perform the ritual on a Wednesday afternoon during a new moon phase. When you receive magickal cash, always donate a small portion of the money to charity. This helps to keep good fortune flowing.

A Spell for Attracting More Money

When funds are getting low, you need to bring out citrine. This sturdy, pale-yellow crystal is thought to not only induce joy and happiness by removing blocks and obstacles from your everyday life; it might also increase financial success and stability.

Materials

> 2 citrine crystals, one larger than the other
>
> A dollar bill or monetary note
>
> An altar or pillar candle, in green, for money, and a candleholder
>
> A paring knife
>
> A few drops of lemon essential oil

Ritual

Cleanse and empower your crystals (see chapter 2, pages 29–35). On a Wednesday afternoon, when the moon is in a new phase, place your monetary note on the altar. Take your candle and, with a knife, inscribe your full name and the words *money* and *abundance* into the wax. Add a few drops of the lemon essential oil to the tip of your finger and anoint the candle, tracing it lengthways from the top to the bottom. Place your candle in a holder, light it, and situate it on top of the note on your altar. Hold the smaller piece of citrine in one hand and the larger piece in the other. Say the following spell twelve times:

> *"I summon the universe to open its pot of abundance*
> *and shine down its light to me.*
> *The money I need is not for greed."*

After you've recited the spell twelve times, close it by adding *"So mote it be."*

Allow the candle to burn down. Place the monetary note deep in your wallet or purse and don't spend it. This money is now magnetized and will bring cash your way. Keep the larger piece of citrine somewhere in your home. Carry the smaller piece with you in your wallet, a pocket, or a purse.

A Spell for Emergency Money

Everyone has experienced receiving an unexpected bill and being unsure of how to pay it. To safeguard yourself from ever being in this position, make sure that you own a piece of sunstone, which is renowned for working quickly and attracting emergency cash when needed.

Materials

A sunstone

Four votive or tealight candles, in green, for money

A paring knife

A candleholder

Ritual

Cleanse and empower your stone (see chapter 2, pages 29–35). Take one of the green candles and, with the knife, scratch your full name and the exact amount of money you need into the wax. Place the candle in a candleholder and light it. Sit in front of the flame, cupping the sunstone in your hands, and imagine that you are being showered with golden coins and banknotes. Do this meditation for about five minutes. Repeat the following spell three times:

> *"This flame burns bright, and money is in sight,*
> *My luck will grow with this crystal in tow."*

After you've recited the spell twelve times, close it by adding *"So mote it be."* Allow the candle to burn down until it extinguishes itself. Repeat this spell for four consecutive days, using a new green candle each day. This simple candle ritual rarely fails, but you must truly believe that the spell will work.

SPELLS FOR NATURE AND THE ENVIRONMENT

Witches will often be seen tending their gardens or growing all kinds of herbs in pots, either on their windowsills or on a patio. Homegrown herbs that are cultivated especially for spells are thought to give a ritual extra power. Any time or attention given to plants makes them even more special to the final outcome.

A Spell for Helping Your Garden Grow

Perform this spell every year to ensure that your plants are always healthy and blooming. Everything has living energy, including flowers, plants, and trees. Malachite is renowned for sending healing and restorative rays to the earth and assisting plants and trees to be the best that they can be!

Materials

> A malachite stone
>
> Ashes from a sandalwood incense stick
>
> A large gardening pot with soil
>
> Any shrub or houseplant in a nursery pot (any size or variety is suitable)

Ritual

Cleanse and empower your stone (see chapter 2, pages 29–35). On a full moon phase, light a sandalwood incense stick next to your malachite. When the incense has burned down, collect the ashes.

Half fill the gardening pot with soil. Scatter the sandalwood incense ashes in the pot and bury the stone. Plant your shrub or plant in the pot, filling around the edges with more soil as necessary. Say the following spell three times:

"Blossom in width and grow in height,
with the magickal power of malachite,
  Everything now will start to sprout,
climb and flower and then branch out."

After you've recited the spell three times, close it by adding *"So mote it be."* Situate the plant somewhere in the center of your garden or another peaceful space and water it thoroughly. Take care of it as you normally would, allowing the magick to spread throughout your space.

A Spell for Protecting and Connecting with Wildlife

Witches worship the great outdoors and enjoy nothing more than feeling at one and in tune with the birds and the animals. A common practice for witches in the United Kingdom is to spellcast for the protection of the environment. The best crystal to use for this purpose is rainforest jasper. The Green Man is a nature deity often depicted through a sculpture or figurine of a man's face encircled with leaves, branches, and foliage; his main purpose is to protect animals and plants from harm. A Green Man ornament or figurine can be purchased from New Age shops or online.

Materials

- A rainforest jasper stone
- A small Green Man ornament
- A stick of sandalwood incense, to represent nature
- A pot of planted sage, for protection and spiritual cleansing

Ritual

Cleanse and empower your stone (see chapter 2, pages 29–35). This spell is best cast outside, so on a fine day (during any moon phase), prepare an altar using an outdoor surface. Place the ornamental Green Man in the center of your workspace. Rest the piece of jasper on top of him. Position the pot of sage next to the Green Man and light the sandalwood incense. In your own words, ask the archangel Ariel, guardian of wildlife, to send love and protection to your garden or local wildlife; then recite the following mantra seven times:

"Earth, plants, animals and trees, ants, worms, butterflies and bees,
I summon the angels to guard them please,
protection for all and free from disease."

After you've recited the spell seven times, close it by adding *"So mote it be."*
When you have said the spell, push the crystal halfway into the soil of the sage
pot so that it is peeping out. Place the container somewhere at the edge of the
garden or outdoor space and make sure that it is repotted when it outgrows
Its tub. If you don't have an outside area to put it, place it inside by the front door.
The Green Man ornament should be propped up beside the building or fastened
to a wall so that he is looking out over the outdoor space or the front door.

A Spell for Healing the Earth

Many witches are humanitarians and like to do their bit for the planet. One
of the things that is worrying the Wiccan community right now is the use of
plastics and how it affects our oceans and marine life. Using crystal craft is a
powerful and influential way to help heal the environment, though the success
of your spell might come about in strange ways. The spell could radiate
toward politicians or people with the power to change laws, shifting their
mind-set and motivating them into action. Of course, if the world's leaders do
start banding together to end pollution, there will be no proof that it was, in
fact, your spell's doing. But if we all pull together and try, our collective energy
could really make a difference. This spell needs to be cast twice a year.

Materials

> 7 small, clear quartz crystals
>
> A large altar or pillar candle
>
> A small bowl of soil
>
> A dish of rainwater

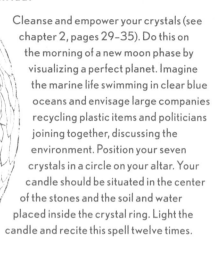

Cleanse and empower your crystals (see chapter 2, pages 29–35). Do this on the morning of a new moon phase by visualizing a perfect planet. Imagine the marine life swimming in clear blue oceans and envisage large companies recycling plastic items and politicians joining together, discussing the environment. Position your seven crystals in a circle on your altar. Your candle should be situated in the center of the stones and the soil and water placed inside the crystal ring. Light the candle and recite this spell twelve times.

*"Protect this planet and all that reside,
animals and humans to stand side by side,
Bring all into balance and heal with your light,
bathe it in beauty in day and at night."*

After you've recited the spell twelve times, close it by adding *"So mote it be."* Let the candle burn for an hour, then blow it out. Take the crystals outside and push them into the ground. If you don't have a garden, you can take them to a woodland and plant them there. You can also toss them into a stream.

Each night light the candle and recite the spell just once. After an hour, blow it out again. Repeat this every night until the candle has burned all the way down.

SPELLS FOR PETS

We all know that animals are far more in tune with the earth than we are, and because of this, it is no coincidence that they respond brilliantly to crystals. They are also drawn to anything magickal; you will notice that cats especially always want to get involved in a spell, even if it's by climbing on the altar and knocking everything off.

A Spell for Healing a Sick Pet

If you think your pet is unwell, they probably are. Animals always play down their symptoms. This comes from their natural instinct to protect themselves from other creatures who might recognize their weakness and become a threat. Before you cast the following spell, make sure to visit your vet and rule out any serious ailments. You don't have to worry too much about the phase of the moon or the day of the week to cast this spell. Always have some yellow candles in the house, though, as healing rituals work better when you burn this color.

Materials

> A small amethyst tumbled stone
>
> A small rose quartz tumbled stone
>
> A votive or tealight candle, in yellow

Ritual

Cleanse and empower your stones (see chapter 2, pages 29–35); when doing so, focus on the stones and believe wholeheartedly that they will alleviate your pet's symptoms. If you know what the illness is, you can inscribe your candles with its name, during any moon phase, and the word *banish*. Wait until your pet is settled, either sleeping or resting, and sit in front of them. Light the candle nearby and take a stone in each hand. In a clockwise motion, circle the stones over your pet's body. Animals react to crystals by twitching slightly. They might show a little movement or they might not, but continue with this healing for about ten minutes or for as long as your pet will allow. When they are calm, recite the following words once:

> *"I summon the Angel Ariel, healer of animals to*
> *bring forth your power and heal my pet.*
> *Remove all pain and suffering from my beautiful companion.*
> *Encircle him/her in your luminous light."*

Then repeat the following three times:

> *"With magick I banish all illness and pain,*
> *let my pet be well again,*
> *Wrap his/her body in restorative rays, heal her/his pain do not delay."*

After you've recited the spell three times, close it by adding *"So mote it be."* Place the stones somewhere near your pet's bed.

A Spell for Bringing a Lost Pet Home

It's heartbreaking and scary when a pet wanders away from home. You can use this spell to encourage them to return unharmed. However, you should also employ good sense and let your neighbors and friends know to keep an eye out for your pet. Create a LOST CAT or LOST DOG flyer that has a picture of your pet. Add information to the pamphlet, such as the area in which your pet was last seen and your phone number. Post on social media. Offer a small reward if you can. The more places you can reach out to, the better. Keep one flyer back to use in your spell.

Materials

    A black tourmaline crystal or tumbled stone

    A photo of your pet or a lost pet flyer

    5 votive or tealight candles, in white

    A few flowers, plants, twigs, or weeds
        from the area around your home
        (or if in the city, a bowl of earth, leaf,
        or flower from your vicinity)

    Your pet's collar or favorite toy

    A pen and piece of paper

    A fireproof dish, or better still,
        an open fire

Ritual

Cleanse and empower your tourmaline (see chapter 2, pages 29–35). Spend at least five minutes empowering it, visualizing your lost pet back in the safety of your care.

Set up a small altar or table and place the photograph or flyer of your pet and the tourmaline in the center. Circle the photo with the five white candles and light them. Place the plant matter around the ring of candles and situate your pet's toy or collar to one side.

Write your pet's name on the top of the paper and then copy out the following spell:

{PET'S NAME},
"Hear me now, hear my plea,
I summon you, return to me.

Walk the path to where I stand, with this magick I command.
No more will you stray or roam;
walk to me and come back home."

Light the candles and recite the words on the piece of paper twelve times. When you have recited the spell twelve times, close it by adding *"So mote it be."* Place the piece of paper and the flyer or photograph in the fireproof dish. Very carefully remove one of the candles and take it outside with the bowl. Light the papers with the flame from the candle and watch the smoke rise into the air. If you have a fireplace, you can burn the paper inside the grate and then go outside to watch the smoke come out of the chimney. Place the candle back on your altar and let all five candles burn down. Finally, place the tourmaline outside on the ground, either by the cat flap or one of the doors.

Hopefully your pet will psychically sense your command and follow the scent of the spell right back to the front door.

A Spell for Communicating with Your Pet

Animals have a language all their own, but while human beings can speak their minds, pets can't. It's alleged that they use a form of telepathy instead. If you have a beloved pet and would like to try to tap into their mind and telepathically communicate with them, use this spell. Jasper and clear quartz are the best crystals for this exercise.

Materials

A piece of jasper or clear quartz

A votive or tealight candle, in blue, for animal communication

Ritual

Cleanse and empower your crystal (see chapter 2, pages 29–35). During any moon phase, sit with your pet on your lap or, for bigger pets, sit on the floor beside them. Tap them gently three times between the ears. Hold the crystal in your left hand while stroking your pet with the other. This will convey the magick to them. Close your eyes and silently talk to them. Tell them you love them and ask for a response. If the magick is working, you will begin to feel a strange tingling sensation engulf your body. You can say as much as you like to your pet. If they have any bad habits, tell them how these make you feel. If it's a particularly bad one that has been driving you insane, ask them to please stop.

This is a personal way you can connect with your pet, so embrace and enjoy this wonderful time together. Stay in this position for as long as your pet is settled. Touching your brow to your pet's forehead can help the messages transmit better. Pay close attention to how you are feeling. Are you sad or excitable? Has some strange thought just popped into your head? This might be a message that your pet is trying to relay to you, so whatever you do, don't brush it off!

A Spell for Stopping "Bathroom" Accidents

You adore your pet, but no amount of love will stop an untrained pet from doing their business all over the house. Messy pets can be a problem, but often, and especially with rescue animals, it can be a sign of stress. Spellcasting with the crystal stibnite can help to change the energy around the home. Hopefully your animal friend will understand that any bathroom duties must be performed outside or in the litter box.

Materials

> A stibnite crystal
>
> A personal item of your pet's, such as a favorite toy
>
> A plastic bag and poop scoop, to represent the problem
>
> A bag of your pet's favorite treats
>
> A votive or tealight candle, in yellow, for calming stress

Ritual

Cleanse and empower your crystal (see chapter 2, pages 29–35). During any moon phase, place the crystal and all the other items on the altar; light the candle and recite the following spell three times:

> *"Cherished pet, I sense your stress, and this is why you make a mess,*
> *With this crystal I bring peace, and all the mishaps soon will cease,*
>
> *From now on when you need to go, in sunshine, wind, rain, or snow,*
> *Use the little box or go outdoors,*
> *Never on the carpets, and not on the floors."*

After you've recited the spell three times, close it by adding *"So mote it be."* Let the candle burn down on its own and put the crystal outside. When your pet does their business properly, reward them with a magickal treat.

SPELLS FOR PROTECTION

Not all protective crystals work in the same way, so choose your stone depending on what you are trying to achieve. Fluorite,for example, is a powerful protection stone that defends against bad dreams and wards off negative people. Black obsidian, on the other hand, helps prevent psychic attacks. See the list of Protection stones in chapter 4 on page 95.

A Spell for Protection When Out and About

Negative energy is everywhere. Every single day brings encounters with people who are feeling low or suffering from depression, are disgruntled and ill-tempered, or are selfish and greedy. Every experience, good or bad, causes a person to unconsciously throw out an emotion. That energy can sometimes engulf your own aura, causing you to empathically inherit emotions of sadness, anger, or indignation. Day-to-day temperaments affect the vibrations we give off, so it is essential to continuously safeguard ourselves.

Fluorite is renowned for being a powerful, protective stone that not only guards against negative vibrations but also acts as a barrier, making any bad energy bounce right off you. This crystal cleanses its user from the outside and from within, so it not only forms a shield around you; it also boosts self-confidence and stabilizes the aura.

When out and about, many witches like to have a piece of fluorite on their person, whether in a wallet, purse, or pocket, or even in a bra. A piece of jewelry, like a ring or a necklace, is convenient.

Materials

A fluorite crystal or piece of fluorite jewelry

2 large white altar candles

A stick of dragon's blood (resin) incense

Ritual

During any moon phase, cleanse and empower your crystal (see chapter 2, pages 29–35). Making sure that the white altar candles are burning, light the incense and place the fluorite in your hand. Hold the crystal over the top of the incense stick and bathe the stone in the smoke. As you do this, recite the following incantation three times:

"All negativity you will detect,
I charge your power to guard and protect,
Encircle me with luminous light,
keep me safe both day and night."

After you've recited the spell three times, close it by adding *"So mote it be."* Place the crystal on the altar. Allow the candles to burn beside it for a few hours, then blow them out.

A Spell for Banishing

 Whether you are expelling evil spirits or trying to remove an unwanted person from your life, using black obsidian alongside osha root creates a powerful combination of magick. Osha, which only attracts spiritual vibrations, is easily purchased online. When combined with the obsidian's superpower, it forms a shield that is difficult to penetrate.

As with any banishing ritual, it is vital that you cast this spell with positive intent. Keep your emotions neutral and try not to allow any negative thoughts into your mind. If you are angry, you might inadvertently create a ball of negativity that could harm the person you wish to banish, or worse —it could attract negativity to you. To keep everyone safe, always banish a person with loving intentions.

Materials

A black obsidian stone

A votive or tealight candle, in black, for banishment

A votive or tealight candle, in white, for attracting protection

Osha root, either a large piece or a collection of smaller pieces

A fireproof bowl

A small piece of paper and a pen

A gardening pot filled with soil

Ritual

Cleanse and empower your crystals (see chapter 2, pages 29-35). This spell is best performed during a new moon phase. When setting up your altar, place the black candle to one side of the table and the white candle to the other; then light them. Put your osha root in the bowl and position it in the altar's center, between the two candles. Lay your obsidian in front of the dish.

On the paper, write in detail about what or who you want to banish. Be specific with your wording.

Example 1:

I am banishing the evil entity from my home.
It will leave my house with immediate effect.

Example 2:

I am banishing {NAME} from my life.
They will leave my presence with immediate effect.
I send them away with love and blessings.
Let nothing harm or hinder them.

Example 3:

I am banishing the bad luck that clings to my life.
I will be free of this with immediate effect.

Place the paper with your written words on the altar and then repeat what you have written out loud seven times. After you've recited the words seven times, close by adding *"So mote it be."* Rest the paper in the bowl over the osha root and, with the black candle, set the paper on fire. (Please be careful when you are doing this.) You should be left with the osha root and the ashes from the written spell in the bowl. When the black and white candles have burned down, take the ashes, osha root, and black obsidian and bury them in the gardening pot. Leave the pot by your front door. You can always plant some flowers in it later to make it look pretty.

A Spell for Protection While Traveling

The beautiful protective energy that malachite offers makes it a perfect charm to carry while traveling. It is exceptionally good for plane journeys and crowded airports. Malachite also has the power to dispel fears, so if you are nervous about flying or have a fear of heights, this is the crystal for you.

Materials

A malachite stone

Your travel paperwork, such as your printed boarding pass or booking form

A votive or tealight candle, in green, for travel

Ritual

Cleanse and empower your stone (see chapter 2, pages 29–35) a few days before you travel. When empowering the malachite, imagine yourself at the airport, train station, or bus station, stone in hand. Visualize white rays of protection radiating from the stone. Envisage yourself again, this time sitting on the plane, train, or bus, still holding the stone. Once again, visualize the white lights brightly emanating from the stone. When you're satisfied that your stone is empowered, place the paperwork on your altar and light the candle. Place the malachite on top of the paperwork and repeat this spell twelve times.

> *"Let your inner light protect me; divine power encircles me.*
> *I am sheltered in your safety; I am at one with this stone."*

After you've recited the spell twelve times, close it by adding *"So mote it be."* Leave the stone next to the burning candle for about an hour, then blow out the candle and save it. The evening before your journey, light the same candle and situate the malachite in front of it. Repeat the incantation another twelve times. Allow the candle to burn for the rest of the evening. Blow it out before bedtime. Carry the stone in your carry-on luggage during both the outbound and the inbound journey.

A Spell for Protection While Driving

So many traffic accidents occur every single day. It's imperative that we protect ourselves and our loved ones when we drive by practicing safe, defensive driving, which can be helped through the use of crystals. For this ritual, we need a protective crystal. The best stone for such a job is turquoise.

Materials

A turquoise stone

A votive or tealight candle, in gold or yellow, for protection

Ritual

Cleanse and empower your crystal (see chapter 2, pages 29–35). During any moon phase, choose a time when the house is quiet and you know you won't be disturbed. Hold the turquoise in your hand and light the candle. Repeat the following incantation seven times:

> *"When I leave and when I arrive, protect me every time I drive.*
> *Sheltered from hazards and jeopardies, avoid the dangers around me."*

(This is a beautiful little prayer mantra that you can memorize and speak every time you get in your vehicle. If you are

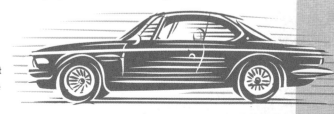

surrounded by people, you can always say it silently in your mind.) After you've recited the spell seven times, close it by adding *"So mote it be."* Allow the candle to burn down.

To complete the ritual, for drivers, place the empowered turquoise underneath the front wheel of your vehicle and leave it there overnight. The next morning, place the stone in the glove compartment, making sure it remains there indefinitely. If you don't drive or own a car, you can place it under a friend's vehicle (with permission) or place it under a bike's wheel. The crystal needs to absorb the energies of transportation, so any mode of transportation will work. Make sure you carry the stone with you on your future journeys and never travel without it.

A Spell for Ending a Curse

Curses really do exist, but they usually feed on a person's fear and so are only effective if you believe that you have been afflicted in some way. There is, however, another kind of curse called the "evil eye." If you make an enemy who is consumed with hateful thoughts toward you, the undesirable energy they conjure can often be transported straight in your direction. This ball of horrible negativity can hit you head-on, and worse still, the perpetrator won't even realize what they're doing!

If you do get infected with the evil eye, you might start to get a run of bad luck or start feeling out of sorts, and this can hang around for as long as the other person is angry with you. This is one of the reasons why witches always try to remain neutral when casting spells; the principal power in a spell stems from our emotions, so it is crucial that, regardless of how annoyed or furious you are, you keep a lid on your feelings.

Try to maintain a healthy mind, because if you are inadvertently directing negativity to someone who is highly protected, the energy you send out could bounce off the other person and come straight back at you!

Materials

    An onyx stone

    1 cup (280 g) of black salt powder

    A plate

    A paring knife

    A long tapered candle, in white

Ritual

Cleanse and empower your crystal (see chapter 2, pages 29–35). In the morning of a waxing moon phase, construct a circle of salt on the plate, leaving no gaps. Place the crystal in the center. With the knife, carefully carve away the wax on the flat end of your candle to expose the wick. When it's done correctly, you should be able to see both ends of the candlewick.

Hold the candle over the top of the plate and light each end of the wick. Don't worry if the wax drips onto the dish. Repeat the following spell seven times:

> *"This candle burns from end to end,*
> *all negative vibes, I avoid.*
> *With this vessel I defend,*
> *this curse is smashed and now destroyed."*

After you've recited the spell seven times, close it by adding *"So mote it be."* Blow out just one end of the candle and push that end onto the center of the plate. It is best to cast this spell when you haven't got anywhere to be, because you must allow the candle to burn all day until it puffs out. When it has burned down, take the now-empowered protective salt and sprinkle it outside your front door. The onyx must remain inside the house for at least two weeks. You should now be entrenched in a beautiful bubble of protection.

SPELLS FOR PSYCHIC AND SPIRITUAL ENHANCEMENT

Most witches are constantly trying to raise their spiritual vibration with the aid of meditation and spellcraft. Doing this is thought to elevate the consciousness, allowing one's psychic awareness to shine through and develop. This section will help you to tap into your psyche and intensify your abilities.

A Spell for Strengthening Psychic Abilities

As with anything, the more you rehearse any type of divination, the better you will become, but you can boost your ability from time to time, making your readings or predictions more successful.

There are quite a few crystals we can use for this purpose, but the best by far is albite. This crystal can be pricey, though, so if it is outside your budget, you might want to choose another from the reference guides in chapter 4 (pages 91–96).

Materials

An albite or corresponding crystal, to boost psychic awareness

A large tall tapered or block candle, in white

A glass bowl

Spring water or rainwater, enough to fill the bowl

Ritual

Cleanse your crystal (see chapter 2, pages 29–35). On the night of a waning moon, sit in a comfortable chair and empower your crystal by holding it on your forehead chakra for about ten minutes. During this time, concentrate on the power of the stone and imagine that it is projecting psychic rays directly into your brain.

Stand in front of your altar and place a lit white candle, to symbolize purity, and a glass bowl filled with the water in the center. Drop the crystal into the bowl, turn off the lights, and gaze into the water for a few minutes. When the water is still, dip your finger into the bowl to create a ripple and then dab your wet finger on your forehead. Say the following spell nine times:

> *"Psychic powers rise within me,*
> *increase my awareness, let me see,*
> *Fill my being with glorious light,*
> *when the moon wanes on this magickal night."*

After you've recited the spell nine times, close it by adding *"So mote it be."* Blow out the candle. Repeat the water-dabbing ritual and relight the candle before you conduct any psychic work or divination.

A Spell for Connecting with a Goddess, Guide, or Angel

During meditation, you might like to try to connect with your own personal goddess, guide, or angel. This spells recommends two stones that might be best, but, as always, if you have difficulty sourcing them, you can substitute by using one of the other crystals listed on page 92 (For Divination and Psychic Awareness) or page 96 (Spiritual Matters).

Materials

A goshenite or titanium quartz crystal

A few sprigs of mint, fresh or dried

1 eucalyptus-mint combination incense stick

Ritual

Cleanse and empower your crystal (see chapter 2, pages 29–35) during any moon phase. Guardian spirits adore the scent of mint, so place some beside your bed during your meditation. Light the incense next to the mint and lie on your bed, holding your chosen crystal in your left hand.

Close your eyes and inhale for three seconds, then exhale for three seconds. Repeat this for about five minutes. While you are doing this, focus on how the stones feel in your hand and try to look out of your third eye, which lies at the center of your forehead. If there is anything that you want to speak to your guide about, now is the time.

After a while, you may feel like your body is floaty and weightless. This is perfectly normal. Don't worry if you fall asleep; your guide will often communicate with you when you are in a slumber state. Keep the crystal on your nightstand and, over the coming days, pay attention to how you are feeling. Spirits often speak to you through your subconscious, so you might feel inspired to try something new.

This meditation can often help your angels and guides set you on your destined path.

A Spell for Heightening Your Instincts

We're big advocates for trusting your instincts, but like most people, there are times when we reject our intuitions and live to regret it afterward. It is so important that you listen to your soul. If something doesn't feel right, or you get a creepy feeling about a person, this is an instinctive warning bell and you must take notice!

Materials

A benitoite crystal

1 whole lemon, to improve concentration

1 bay leaf, to stimulate intuition

A bowl

A votive or tealight candle, in yellow

Spring water or rainwater, enough to fill the bowl

Cotton balls

Ritual

Cleanse and empower your crystal (see chapter 2, pages 29–35). On a full moon, slice the whole lemon in half and place it, along with the bay leaf and crystal, in the bowl. Set this on your altar. Light the candle next to the bowl and recite the following spell three times:

"I perceive my truth, my inner voice, the facts I heed I won't misread."

After you've recited the spell three times, close it by adding *"So mote it be."* While the candle is burning, pour the water into the bowl and allow everything to steep until the candle has burned down. Drain just the water into a clean container and put it in the fridge. Every day, drench a cotton ball with the magickal water and place it against the center of your forehead for a few seconds. This potion should last for at least a month.

Create Your Own Crystal Spells

The spells listed in this chapter and throughout this book cover lots of eventualities, but life has a habit of throwing us unusual problems from time to time. When this happens, we may be faced with having to devise a spell of our own.

The magick lies within each one of us, and we are all capable of putting together our own rituals. It is recommended that, once you become more familiar with Wicca, you try to concoct your own magick.

All you need is the basic knowledge of how to cast a spell. This book, along with the other books in the Modern-Day Witch series, gives you a wealth of information, from how to set up an altar to using corresponding items that will influence your spell.

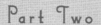

Part Two

EXPLORE MORE CRYSTAL MAGICK

Chapter 6

Crystals and the Moon

THE MOON IS A CONSTANT IN OUR WORLD—SOMETHING MANY of us never give much thought to, and yet, its impact on our earthly lives is profound. The moon, just like everything around us, has energy. It manipulates the ocean's tides through its gravitational pull, which in turn affects countless life forms, including humans. Adult bodies are composed of about two-thirds water, and, although scientists debate this point regularly, the moon's cyclical pull could affect us directly.

You've no doubt heard references to the colorful characters who come out in full force during the full moon. Nurses who work in labor-and-delivery units swear that more babies are born during this time (although science has disproven this claim), and emergency room personnel will testify that it's a batten-down-the-hatches night whenever there's a full moon.

People of all ages tend to sleep less and feel more energetic during this time. Some fishermen study moon charts and base their efforts on the phases of the moon. It is said that fish bite best in the days leading up to the full moon and then again during the dark moon, when the moon is not visible to us.

In short, there is no question that the moon and its phases have a broad influence on the world around us, in everything we see as well as in the energy we feel. To understand how to best use crystals in conjunction with the moon's strength, we need to discuss this topic a bit more. If you are looking to work with crystals in conjunction with the moon to achieve a specific goal, it's a good bet that it's been studied—or at least discussed and debated.

MOON PHASE MAGICK

The moon is entirely predictable; its phases repeat month after month, year after year, in a 29½-day "lunar cycle." It has also been studied by all sorts, both spiritual and scientific, so we have a lot of information on which phases are best for certain purposes.

New

This is the first phase of the moon, often called the crescent moon, in which the moon is emerging from its dark phase in a bare sliver of light. This is the time to focus on new ideas or activities or on anything that has to do with your future. Cast out thoughts or issues that have been nagging away at you, like lost opportunities or broken relationships. Focus on what's coming next. If you want to change your path in life, spells cast during this phase work best.

Waxing

When the moon is waxing before a full moon, its lit portion appears to be growing in size (to the human eye, anyway). This moon phase is associated with intentions that call for an increase or improvement in something. Perhaps you want a raise at work or your relationship with your significant other has been a little stale. Now is the time to give all those mundane things in your life an extra boost.

Full

When the moon is full, it's a good time for concentrating on what your intuition is telling you. It's also a good time for rituals that need an abundance of effort or energy, or for anything that requires diligence on your part. The moon at this time releases power relating to love and relationships, so it is an exceptionally good phase if you need to shed any negative attitudes or if you want to attract more love and romance into your life. It is also excellent for tapping into your creative abilities. It is worth mentioning that animals, especially cats, act up and misbehave during full moon phases, so this would also be a good time for casting spells related to the animal kingdom.

Waning

After the full moon, we see the waning phase, which means we see the moon appearing to shrink in size. This is a good time for meditations that ask for a decrease in whatever area you're focused on—maybe work has been too stressful or you want to lose weight. If you are experiencing a problematic time in your life, the waning phase makes way for clearing out negativity.

Dark of the Moon

During the dark moon phase, the moon is not visible to us. This time takes place after the waning moon and lasts a day or two. On a calendar that tracks moon phases, it usually appears as a dark spot. The dark moon is a time to slow things down for a little while, to focus on yourself and do a little soul-searching.

Other Useful Phases

We've talked about the phases of the moon that you hear discussed with regularity, but what about some of those different phases that come around a little less often?

A **SUPERMOON** occurs when the full moon coincides with the moon's closest approach to Earth during its orbit, about three or four times a year. Its appearance is larger and brighter than during an average full moon, which in turn means that the energy we can harness when casting a spell is also magnified! Love spells cast at this time have a very high success rate.

On the other hand, a **MINIMOON** is when a full moon is farthest from the Earth during its orbit. It's difficult for us to determine merely by looking at it that the moon is in a mini phase, but this also occurs just once every year or so. This phase is unlikely to boost your energy and intention, so keep that in mind if you are planning a mediation concerning something especially important. You may need to pull out some extra crystals to amplify the energy surrounding you.

A **BLUE MOON** refers not to the color, but to a second full moon in a calendar month (or the third of four full moons in a season). Because this occurrence comes around so rarely, its energy is thought to be hyper-focused and powerful. It is believed to double the amount of power that you would ordinarily find on a full moon phase, so any spell that incites long-term results is best performed at this time

A **LUNAR ECLIPSE** is a magickal event when the sun, earth, and moon are perfectly aligned and the moon passes through the earth's shadow. It is thought that any kind of magick, whatever the spell, cast at this time is all-powerful, so it is an opportunity not to be missed.

THE BEST CRYSTALS FOR MOON MAGICK

So now that you know about the moon's phases and their related energy, what kind of crystals work best for bringing your intentions to fruition in the light (or dark) of the silvery moon? You will learn more about crystals, their energies, and their healing properties as you read this book. Some readers likely have gems that they already use with good results. These suggestions are certainly not the be-all and end-all of crystals that can be used in lunar magick.

Moonstone

Of course, this is the primary stone, named because it works so well with the moon's power. This stone can be used during any phase of the moon, and it comes in a variety of colors, including gray, blue, orange, brown, pink, yellow, and green, with sheens ranging from white to bluish-white to silver. It can also appear to be colorless. Moonstone is tied to feminine energy, which makes it a protective and nurturing stone, but it's also connected to anything psychic, so it's terrific if you want to unlock your abilities.

Moonstone is suitable for fresh starts and promotes a sense of stability and calm in one's life. It's said to boost creative thought and energies and help bolster success. As such, it would be best to use this during a waxing moon, which, as discussed on page 188, is the phase that brings about an increase in positive intentions.

Keep this stone close when you're heading into a job interview or thinking about changing career paths. It would also be useful if you must come up with some stellar ideas for teambuilding at work, home renovations, or family-related activities.

Labradorite

A close relative of moonstone (sometimes even called rainbow moonstone), this iridescent crystal is said to increase your intuition and open your Third Eye Chakra, providing the deepest kind of insight and even psychic visions! This is a stone of strength and perseverance. It has protective elements, as it can prevent your positive energy from leaking or escaping. It is most often used to help increase spiritual awareness. Imagine the power of this stone under a supermoon. Nothing would be off-limits to you during that time!

Clear Quartz

Quartz is the workhorse of the crystal realm, as there are dozens of varieties that can (and are) used for virtually every intention and purpose under the sun—or, in this case, under the moon. But don't be misled into thinking clear quartz is nothing special. The reason it's used so frequently is because it works so well with so many different energies. It will help you to either amplify or let go of an issue. It clears up confusion and energy blockages and protects against negative vibes.

This is one stone that would work well under a waning moon, which is a time to focus on decreasing and releasing things that just aren't working out well in your life.

Selenite (Gypsum)

Selenite is named for Selene, the Greek goddess of the moon, which makes it an especially good choice for working under lunar rays. This transparent crystal works well no matter what your intention may be. It provides a powerful force to fight against negative energy and charges everything in its field with good vibes! You can achieve your highest self, clear blockages in your chakras, and pull in powers that are useful and protective. Selenite also promotes a sense of personal honesty and revelations to the self.

REENERGIZING YOUR CRYSTALS
UNDER THE MOON

Like anything that emits energies, crystals need charging now and then for them to continue to work the way we expect them to. We discussed in chapter 2 a few different ways to charge them. Leaving them outside overnight, under the light of a full moon, will reenergize even the hardest-working crystal.

If you decide that this is the method for you, you might like to give your crystals an extra boost by conducting a Lunar Charging Ritual. You can do this ritual with any crystal jewelry that you own as well.

Lunar Charging Ritual

Take your crystals and a blanket outside during a full moon phase. Find a spot where you can clearly see the moon and place the blanket on the ground. Sit on the blanket and place all your crystals in a circle around you. If you only have a few and not enough to form a circle, don't worry; place them in front of you or to either side. If you can, cross your legs. If not, sit with your legs out in front of you. Clasp your hands together and stare up at the moon in the sky. Repeat the following incantation thirteen times.

> *"I call the goddess to attune and cast out power*
> *from the magickal moon.*
> *Bathe these crystals in your light, project your power*
> *through the night."*

If the weather permits, you can sit outside with your crystals for as long as you like, but when you're ready to venture indoors, leave the stones outside. For city dwellers, leave them on the outside of a window ledge in your home or somewhere near an open window. Collect them in the morning.

The next morning, when you bring them inside, don't be surprised if they feel a little different to the touch. Sit quietly, hold each one, and feel the pure energy they emit.

Think about the kind of energy you want each crystal to provide for you. Is it peace? Love? Intuition? Consider this for each crystal you've charged. If you're using them in rituals with clients, you may want to charge them with a healing intention.

Chapter 7

Crystals for Divination

DIVINATION IS THE ART OF CONNECTING WITH THE spirits or the universe (or whatever you call your greater life force) to gain wisdom, insight, and knowledge that may otherwise not be readily available. In other words, this connection may provide information that you can't find on the internet, in a book, or by asking someone else. You could be seeking knowledge related to a specific issue, or you might want a general idea of where things are heading or what action to take.

There are hundreds of forms of divination, dating back thousands of years. Most require a relatively simple setup and low-tech equipment, such as table salt (which we know is actually tiny crystals). We will talk about this at some length later in this chapter (see page 216–17).

Other, more complex forms of divining can be enhanced by adding crystals to the mix, and we will discuss some of those methods, too.

EXPLORING CRYSTAL DIVINATIONS

Even if you've been divining for years, you can always add something unique by using certain stones to enhance your practice.

Some of the best crystals to have on hand for any sort of divination include:

AMETHYST Useful for opening the Third Eye Chakra and expanding one's psychic abilities

AZURITE Also works with the Third Eye and Throat Chakras to promote clairvoyance, insight, and psychic vision

BERYL Enhances its user's abilities during any divination

BLOODSTONE Expands clairvoyance and encourages lucid dreaming

CALCITE Promotes astral travel and journeying to other realms

FLUORITE Works with the third eye to bring clarification to psychic visions

IOLITE Enhances all forms of supernatural powers

KYANITE Often used in wand formation; increases the powers of perception, intuition, and channeling spiritual styles and messages

LABRADORITE One of the workhorse crystals; collaborates with one's highest energy and enhances every psychic skill

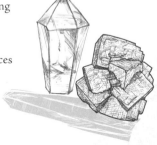

LAPIS LAZULI Used for protection from dark forces while channeling psychic power; opens the third eye to enhance psychic visions

MOONSTONE Works best during the full moon, to expand intuition; useful when scrying with black mirrors (see page 42)

OBSIDIAN Enhances one's connection to the spirit world during scrying and improves psychic vision

QUARTZ Enhances the highest form of energy and protects against dark forces

SAPPHIRE All colors can be used to expand intuition, astral travel, and third eye vision

SODALITE Improves perception and understanding of psychic messages

TURQUOISE Enhances communication between its user and their spirit guides/universal forces

These are some of the best crystals to use with divination, but you can always turn to the "For Divination and Psychic Awareness" section of chapter 4, (page 92) for further inspiration. You may find that there is one stone you genuinely feel a strong connection with, so if this is the case, go ahead and incorporate it into your session!

For all the divination methods discussed in this section, you may want to keep a journal of your observations and make note of which crystals you have used in your Book of Shadows.

Crystallomancy

Of course we're going to start this discussion by talking about the crystal ball. In ancient times, people gazed upon any reflective surface as a means of telling the future. Surfaces included water, knife blades, pools of ink, ice, and even fingernails that had been buffed to a shine—all of which were accessible to the ordinary person. Crystal balls were another story— they were expensive and used only by wealthy families.

At that time, people believed that crystals were permanently frozen water and, as such, were infused with magick. Well, they were on the right track— even though crystals are not representative of a deep freeze, they are, of course, magick in the palm of your hand!

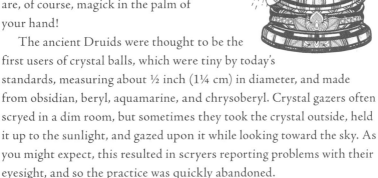

The ancient Druids were thought to be the first users of crystal balls, which were tiny by today's standards, measuring about ½ inch (1¼ cm) in diameter, and made from obsidian, beryl, aquamarine, and chrysoberyl. Crystal gazers often scryed in a dim room, but sometimes they took the crystal outside, held it up to the sunlight, and gazed upon it while looking toward the sky. As you might expect, this resulted in scryers reporting problems with their eyesight, and so the practice was quickly abandoned.

During the time of the Druids, crystal ball gazing was often used in magickal ceremonies and to reveal the secrets of the past. This included the purification and blessing of the sphere by a magician who would anoint it with a unique blend of olive oil. Typically, a young boy (a representation of purity of mind) was called upon to do the scrying, and he would report seeing a spirit in the ball if the reading was a success.

These days, crystal balls are usually made of quartz, and experts in crystallomancy recommend using one that has at least a 2½-inch (6 cm) diameter, so that any images that appear are easier to see. If you're shopping for a ball this size, you should be aware of two things:

1. They can be quite expensive.

2. They usually include imperfections called *veils*, which are normal and will not affect your ability to see images during a scrying session.

Before using your crystal ball, you'll need to cleanse it. Choose one of these three methods:

1. Place a new washcloth or dishtowel in the bottom of your sink. Place your ball on top and run warm water over it. Imagine any negative energy being washed away in this gentle bath.

2. Put your crystal ball in a bowl of salt overnight. The salt will absorb dark energy. Make sure to discard the salt afterward.

3. Hold the ball in your hand and waft sage incense all around it.

Whenever you see a movie with a crystal gazer, the person will inevitably have a giant sphere placed on a stand in front of them. In real life, the ball is smaller and can be held on a piece of black velvet in the scryer's hands. (If you do have a stand for your crystal ball, make sure you place the stand itself on top of a piece of black velvet during your reading.) Scrying is best done at night, ideally during the full moon or the nights leading up to it (aka the waxing moon phase).

Prepare a quiet space for yourself that is free of distractions. Make this space as open to the spirit world and the universe as possible. You can light candles, burn incense, or scatter crystals of your choosing around your workspace.

The key to successful crystal ball gazing is one part focus and one part relaxation. You must focus during your preparation, when you are forming your question. The ball is a good source of information concerning the past, present, or future, so you can ask it virtually anything. Once you have the question in mind, you want to let your mind soften and even blur as much as possible—this is the relaxation. Now gaze into your crystal, continuing to let your mind open. Breathe deeply and know that you will see images related to your question.

Here's what you can expect during a successful session:

1. A cloud will appear in the center of the ball, indicating that spiritual energy is taking hold. It is usually white, but it may change colors.

2. The cloud will eventually fade to darker gray or black.

3. Images related to your query might appear next and in quick succession. Don't be alarmed—just take it all in.

4. The images will eventually fade into a mist before disappearing.

Once the fog has dissipated, wrap your crystal ball in the velvet cloth and set it aside. Now, in your Book of Shadows or journal, write down what you saw in the ball, whether or not it makes sense.

To recharge your crystal ball, place it in the moonlight overnight. Allow twenty-four hours between scrying sessions.

As a final point, it is worth mentioning that when the ball is not in use, it is always best to cover it with a piece of white, gold, or purple velvet.

> Please always refrain from placing your ball in direct sunlight; crystal balls have been known to cause fires.

Crystal Pendulums

The swing of the pendulum can offer insight and wisdom regarding any number of issues.

Many pendulums consist of a simple weight at the bottom of a chain, but *dowsing*, or divining with a crystal fixed to the pendulum's end, allows more focused energy to exchange between you and the spirit world. The type of crystal you should use depends mainly on your question. If you want to find out more about your love life, choose a pendulum with a rose quartz tip. For money matters, opt for some green jade or perhaps a garnet. For general questions, a clear quartz is perfect. There are many crystal pendulums to be found online, all created with a multitude of different crystals attached.

Some of the most popular pendulum crystals include:

AMETHYST, OBSIDIAN, LAPIS LAZULI
Encourage psychic energy, balance, and peace

CITRINE Fosters abundance and prosperity

FLUORITE Encourages a clear and organized mind

HEMATITE Grounds and protects from negative energies

HONEY CALCITE, RUBY Both promote positive energy for personal goals

ROSE QUARTZ Promotes healing energies, both physical and emotional

SELENITE Encourages psychic energy and mental clarity

SMOKY QUARTZ Protects from dark energy and encourages grounding and prosperity

When using a pendulum, either questions must be appropriate for a *yes* or *no* response, or you can create a chart of potential answers to hold under the pendulum. It's advisable to start out with yes-or-no questions, so you can get to know your pendulum and its nuances.

Holding the pendulum takes some practice, as you need a steady hand. It's easy to set the pendulum swinging by holding it too loosely, and you want to make sure you're channeling answers from spirits—not from the flick of your wrist! If your pendulum has a long chain, your hand motion is more likely to set it swinging by accident. Try adjusting the length of the chain, making it shorter for tighter control.

Every pendulum has its own personality. Some of them are very responsive, while others are quieter and come off as rather shy.

Oh, they will give you a definitive answer, but you must read between the lines.

Things to observe with your pendulum:

- Does it swing back and forth, or does it move in a circular motion?
- If it has a circular motion, is clockwise indicative of a YES or a NO? (Counterclockwise obviously means the opposite.)
- Does the pendulum come to a dead stop to indicate an answer of UNCLEAR or MAYBE, or does it slow down?
- Is it always responsive to easy questions, or is there a time of day when it seems to work best?

In this phase, when you're learning about how your pendulum communicates, keep your questions simple with yes-or-no answers that are known to you. For example:

- Is my name Susan?
- Is today Monday?
- Do I like chocolate?
- Am I allergic to bees?
- Is it raining right now?

Jot down anything that seems quirky or noteworthy about your pendulum in your Book of Shadows so you can track patterns of communication.

Talking to Your Pendulum

What kind of questions can you ask your pendulum? There is nothing off-limits, but this is one instance where you'll need to be very clear about what you want to know *before* you begin, or else you may end up more confused. Questions should not be open-ended. For example, you can't ask your pendulum what your future mate looks like—that requires a more detailed answer than the pendulum can provide. However, you can still get that information by rephrasing and asking several questions:

- Does my future mate have brown hair?
- Do they have blue eyes?
- Are they tall?
- Are they taller than I am?
- Do I already know this person?

And, depending on the answers, of course, you can ask follow-up questions. (For example, let's say this person doesn't have brown hair, according to the pendulum. Okay then, is it blond? Is it red? Is this person bald?)

The other way to get information involves creating a chart to place under your pendulum. In the case of asking about a future mate's physical appearance, first make a list of attributes, such as various eye, hair, and skin colors; heights; age ranges; etc. Now make a pie chart with one "slice" representing each potential answer. Hold the pendulum above your chart and ask it to indicate what color eyes this person has. Next ask about hair, then height. Now you've got a pretty good idea of who the universe has in mind for you!

You can get some detailed information with your pendulum, whether you're using a chart or simply asking questions. It takes time, practice, and patience, but regular pendulum users swear it's worth the effort! Don't forget to cleanse and charge your crystal pendulum every now and then (see chapter 2, pages 29–35), especially if you've had a long or particularly involved session.

Crystal Tarot Readings

The classic tarot deck has seventy-eight cards and contains four suits: wands, pentacles, cups, and swords. These four suits are known as the Minor Arcana and each includes court cards, comprising kings, queens, knights, and pages. There are fifty-six suit cards in total. The remaining twenty-two cards are referred to as the Major Arcana. Readings can be "cold," meaning that there is no specific issue being addressed, or they can be more focused, with the reader concentrating on a particular question in mind from the start. When you become proficient in the art of tarot reading, you can either read the cards for yourself or you can perform a translation for someone else.

One factor to keep in mind with the cards is that, although they each have particular significance, they can mean something entirely different when placed next to other cards in a spread. Some readers learn their skill from studying books, whereas others prefer to gain inspiration from the pictures on the cards. This is referred to as a "psychic reading."

Before bringing your cards out, prepare a crystal workspace. You can select crystals that you regularly work with or choose several from the list at the beginning of this chapter. Place the stones around the area where you will be performing your reading.

If you are carrying out a reading for yourself, then to begin, you must shuffle your deck for around three minutes. While you are doing this, focus on the questions you might have.

Because each card has multiple meanings (depending on whether it's drawn upright or reversed), it's perfectly acceptable for the cards to be mixed up every which way. After a good shuffle, split the deck into three equal piles with your left hand, then choose one of the three piles to work with before setting the other two piles to one side. Place the crystal(s) at the top of the workspace. Spread the cards out in a fan-like manner and, using any hand, select your cards. Try these simple layouts for tarot beginners:

THREE-CARD SPREAD: This is the most straightforward layout, but it can still give you useful information. This layout comprises only three cards, representing (from left to right): the past and influences affecting the current situation; the current situation; and the future.

FIVE-CARD SPREAD: This is the three-card spread, but with two additional cards—one placed above, and one below, so that the layout resembles a cross. The card placed below signifies the causes of the current situation, and the card above represents the action to resolve it.

HORSESHOE SPREAD: This is a seven-card spread in the shape of a semicircle. From left to right, the cards represent:

- The past
- The present
- Hidden influences
- The *querent*, or person having the reading
- Attitudes of the people surrounding the querent
- The action the querent should take
- The outcome

After the cards are in place, you can hold a crystal in one or both hands to help connect with your psychic vision. When you're done reading for someone else, you can cleanse yourself with a kyanite or selenite wand by simply waving it from top to bottom of your body while envisioning a white light coming to clear any lingering energies.

When you are finished with your cards, you can cleanse and charge them along with your crystals. Just place a large crystal, like quartz, moonstone, amethyst, or kyanite, on top of the deck and then put it out in the moonlight overnight.

Tarot magick is a relatively new practice but one fast becoming very popular due to its pinpoint accuracy. It tends to be more effective in conjunction with crystals. Once you have learned the simple meanings of all seventy-eight cards, you can place a card on your altar that represents your situation, resting it underneath the crystal of your choice before performing your ritual. For example, if you wanted to boost your cash flow, you would choose the best financial card in the deck (aka the Ace of Pentacles) and place it on your altar along with any other items needed in your spell. Or, when performing spells for luck and happiness, you would select the two best cards in the deck for those attributes (the Sun and the Ace of Cups) and rest them on the altar underneath the chosen crystals.

A Cup of Crystal Tea

Tea leaf reading, or tasseography, is an ancient Chinese practice that you can incorporate into your crystal work. You will need boiling-hot water, loose tea leaves, a mug or teacup, a deep saucer or small bowl, and the crystal of your choice.

Start by pouring the water into a cup and adding loose tea leaves. Some experts say to add just a pinch; others recommend a tablespoon. You can adjust the amount based on how your initial sessions go.

Let the tea cool so that it's not scalding, then place the crystal of your choosing into the cup.

This should be a time of total relaxation for you, so make it as peaceful as possible. Light a fire or snuggle up in a blanket if it's a cold day, or listen to some soothing music. Now think about the issue you'd like to gain clarity around. Don't overthink it; just put the thought or question in your mind and let it swirl around as the tea leaves steep.

After five minutes, carefully remove the crystal (use a pair of tongs or a spoon if the liquid is still very hot) and set it aside. Swirl the tea in the cup three times in a clockwise direction, and then slowly pour the liquid into the saucer or bowl. Now look inside the cup at the trail of tea leaves left behind. Hold your crystal in your hand while you do the reading for added understanding.

Start your reading at the handle of the cup (the handle represents the person whose fortune is being read). This is your chance to interpret the shapes as you see fitting.

- **Images to the right of the handle represent things that might take place in the future.** Example: The tea leaves form into the shape of a couple holding hands, so the querent might be soon embarking on a new relationship.

- **Images to the left represent things that have happened previously.** Example: You may observe the image of a plane, so the person might have just come back from a trip.

- **Shapes close to the handle are signs relating to the querent's present circumstance.** Example: You could see the shape of a sad face, which would symbolize the querent having battled with life for a period.

- **Images near the top third of the cup show events that will transpire right away.** Example: If you see something that resembles a dollar sign, it might mean unexpected money is coming the querent's way.

- **Shapes in the middle third of the vessel represent events that will occur soon.** Example: The leaves might give the appearance of a cat or a dog, so a pet might be giving cause for concern to the owner in the next week or so.

- **Images on the bottom of the cup usually indicate things that will arise in the coming months.** Example: You might view wings or clouds so you would predict that the querent will be guided by the spirit world.

It's also a good idea to write your observations in a journal or your Book of Shadows—including the type of crystal you used—so that you can look back later and remember the reading.

Crystal Mirror Divination

Mirrors are frequently featured in fairy tales and mystical stories, often representing a veil between two worlds or a device that grants its owner magickal abilities. Think of Snow White's evil stepmother, the Queen, asking, "Who's the fairest of them all?" The mirror not only told her that Snow White was still alive; it also said Snow White was more even more beautiful that the Queen herself. Another example can be found in *Alice's Adventures in Wonderland*, where a young girl steps through a mirror to a fantastical world. Everything Alice experienced was just on the other side of that reflective surface, alive and well the whole time. In yet another example, in stories about the wizard Merlin of Arthurian legend, he is often said to possess a magickal mirror that let him see anywhere in the realm.

A mirror can also capture our souls—or lack thereof. In lore, vampires have no reflection, and some cultures reject the use of mirrors because of a belief that it may alter or damage the soul. Breaking a mirror is supposed to cause you seven years' bad luck, but why? This probably has to do with the belief that our souls can be contained in a mirror's reflection, and breaking the mirror causes the soul to scatter somewhat.

When Jews practice the seven-day mourning ritual of sitting shiva, mirrors in the home are covered. One reason for this is to reflect on grief without focusing on one's physical appearance. Kabbalists, however, believe that a time of grief is ripe for the dark energies of anger, regret, and guilt to enter a home through a mirror's surface.

Mirrors also show us the absolute reality of our world—or at least what is visible to the naked eye. In this book we focus more on what *isn't* readily apparent to us. That's where our crystal mirror divination comes in.

Black Obsidian Mirror Scrying

To practice a crystal mirror divination, we're going to talk first about the magickal black mirror, which is the gold standard for mirror scrying. These mirrors are usually constructed from black obsidian. They are prepared for use with a special cleansing ritual before being fused together and rubbed with an herbal blend that attracts and holds the highest amount of spiritual energy.

To charge your mirror, you must leave it outside to bathe under the light of a full moon. City dwellers can leave the mirror on a windowsill. The window should be left open, either fully or partly, depending on the weather.

Place a moonstone and something made from gold on the surface; this helps to really empower the mirror. (Remember that the moonstone is noted for its qualities of intuition, magick, mysticism, dream activation, lucid dreaming, serenity, positive insight, and protection.)

The black scrying mirror has many uses in the world of magick, including:

- Connection to spirit guides

- Augmenting wisdom and knowledge (aka deepening your connection to the spiritual and seeking more profound connections and knowing)

- Access to Akashic records (a collection of all thoughts, emotions, intentions, knowing, words, prayers, and actions that have ever or will ever occur, according to the nineteenth-century Russian occultist Helena Blavatsky. They exist on an etheric plane and are accessible only through spiritual connection)

- Astral projection and travel, or the manner of one's spirit leaving the body and experiencing other dimensions, realms, and spiritual planes

- Divination of the future

- Self-healing and meditation

- Transmission of information to spiritual realms

Although your black mirror can be used at any time, regular scryers say that their mirrors—not unlike other magickal tools—tend to work best during a full moon. You don't have to worry too much, though; you can use your mirror during any moon phase—it will still work.

Magickal mirrors are used quite differently from the average looking glass. For one, they're used in the dark. Many black mirrors come with stands, but you can also place the mirror on a flat surface or in the palm of your hand for scrying. You can light a candle and place teh mirror to the side of the mirror or behind it (if your mirror is on a stand), or in the moonlight, as discussed previously. You want your mirror's surface to be a blank, dark canvas, as though you are looking into a tunnel or portal.

Make sure the mirror's surface is clean. You can wipe it with a soft cloth and a little rubbing alcohol to remove smudges. Although you aren't using the mirror to see in the most literal sense, you don't want anything on its surface to distract you.

Place your mirror in its intended place, making sure it's stable and visible to you. This sounds obvious, but again, once you are engaged in this process, you don't want anything to break your focus. Don't, for example, lean a large mirror on an object that may fall midway through your session.

To prepare for this ritual, first take a cleansing shower or bath. You should also prepare your space ahead of time so that it's ready to go when you are. You can incorporate the black mirror into a crystal grid (see pages 222–29), or you can use it by itself. Now let's begin scrying:

1. **Close your eyes and imagine both you and the mirror in a protective white light.** The light swirls and encircles you from top to bottom. Maybe it shimmers; maybe there is a star included in its beams. Allow the light to enter your chakras, from top to bottom, infusing your being with harmony and peace.

2. **Place your hands at the sides of your mirror and let that light transfer into it.** You may move your hands up and down the edges of the mirror, but avoid touching the surface. When you feel the charge is complete, bring the light back to your own being.

3. **Now close your eyes and breathe deeply.** Concentrate on any tense areas in your body, like your neck, your back, or your shoulders. Feel your ribs expand with each inhalation and imagine your lungs deflating fully during your exhalation. Continue to do this until you feel you are fully relaxed and able to engage with the spiritual plane. The goal is to put yourself into a light trance.

4. **Repeat your intention to yourself, being as specific as you can.** This is a good time to connect with a spirit or the universe, to appeal for guidance. You can call on your guides with a simple incantation, something like *"I ask {SPIRIT} to guide me toward the answers I am seeking. I ask that you help visions come to me unhindered and completely."*

5. **With your question in mind, open your eyes and gaze into the mirror, using it as a focal point for the visions coming to mind.** This is kind of like focused daydreaming—the difference being that you are aware of the images coming to your mind. Let the visions wander where they will—you do not need to have control over them, nor should you try to direct them. This can be difficult for someone who likes to be in charge, but right now, a spirit is sending the signals—so sit back and just receive.

6. **When you feel that the apparitions are slowing or have come to a clear conclusion, close your eyes again.** Stretch your neck to the left, right, front, and back, and slowly bring yourself back to full alertness. Give gratitude to your spirit guides for what you've seen and experienced.

7. **Reach for your journal or Book of Shadows and pen and write down what you've experienced.** Put everything on the page, even if it doesn't make sense to you right now. Confusing images might take on a new meaning during any future scrying sessions or during your daily interactions.

It may be tempting to dive into a black mirror divination daily, especially if you currently have a major life issue around which you're seeking clarity. However, make sure you give yourself enough time between sessions to process your visions. You don't want to end up confusing or overwhelming yourself!

Crystal Salt Readings

Halomancy (or *alomancy*) is the art of reading the future with salt. Salt has a long history of being connected to magickal practices. In ancient times, it was scarce and precious, so it is no wonder that, over the centuries, the superstition of spilling salt was considered bad luck. The only way to counteract the ill fortune was to throw a little of it over your left shoulder, so as to blind the devil standing there.

Even today, ancient practices of using salt for purification, protection, and consecration are continued. For example, salt is used to cleanse crystals and energy fields. When you take a cleansing bath prior to a

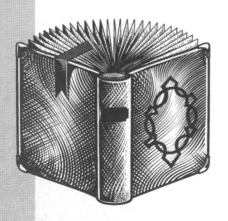

ritual, it's recommended that you toss in a handful of Epsom salts to draw negative energy from your aura. And many practitioners of all sorts of magick sprinkle salt in each corner of the room in which they are casting a spell or performing a ritual. This prevents negative energies from entering the space.

There are several ways to use salt to divine your future:

1. **Sprinkle salt on a flat surface, like a table, and then observe the images that form.** Ridges of salt indicate rough times ahead, while dips and waves in the salt represent obstacles to overcome. If the salt lands in a level pattern, it means that everything is going to be just fine.

2. **Casting salt into a fire is a type of pyromancy.** The idea is to read the images in the sparks created by the salt hitting the flames.

3. **Another type of salt reading is a little like reading tea leaves.** Create a salt solution (¼ teaspoon of salt to 1 tablespoon of liquid should do the trick) and swirl it around a container. If you're using a salt-and-water solution, we recommend placing it in a teacup with a dark interior so that the images can be easily seen. Set it aside and allow the liquid to evaporate, then study the salt left within.

The images you see during halomancy are indicative of your immediate future, making it an easy, inexpensive, and quick way to see what's coming into your life!

Aleuromancy

The practice of using salt to read the future likely started with a different form of divination: aleuromancy, or the use of flour for fortune-telling. In this practice, dough is mixed and separated into balls. If salt is available, it's added to the mix. Sacred symbols are written on slips of paper, added into the dough balls, and baked, in the same way that we now bake fortune cookies. Querents seeking psychic guidance each choose one dough ball, and a diviner determines the person's future based on the size and shape of the dough ball in conjunction with the symbol baked inside.

ENHANCE YOUR PSYCHIC ABILITIES

When we talk about psychic skills, we are talking about the ability to process input and information that is all around us all the time. Some of this information is visible and obvious, while other signs are subtle and easily missed. We are all born with a sensitive intelligence and enough spirituality to process intangible universal cues, but as we age, most of us become focused on other things happening in our daily lives and lose our belief in the energies that we can't see.

Intuition is strongly linked to our psychic ability, and both are useful in divination. Again, we are all born with an inner voice that tells us when a situation or person is good, bad, or dangerous, but with time, many of us tune out that voice and try to reason our way through life. While reason certainly has its place, it does fall short sometimes. Think about a time when you just knew someone was lying to you but you couldn't prove it, or when you met a person for the first time and took an immediate dislike to them. In the absence of actual evidence to validate your feelings, you reasoned, *This person must be telling the truth* or *Everyone else thinks this person is fabulous, so it must be me*. And then, of course, the truth was eventually exposed, and you learned that your intuition was right! Never ignore your feelings. If a thought pops into your head, it must be for a reason.

Fortunately, intuition is never really lost. In fact, it's rather easily recovered with a little effort. Once your intuition is up and running, we can dig into some crystal psychic tricks!

Listening to Intuition

To reacquaint yourself with your inner voice, you need to give yourself the time and space to actually hear it. A few crystals can really help unlock your hidden intuition; choose one of the following:

- **Benitoite**
- **Euclase**
- **Kyanite**
- **Moonstone**
- **Hollandite**

Find a quiet spot where you can sit or lie comfortably for ten to fifteen minutes, and cup your crystal in your hands. Think about an issue in your life that is causing some confusion (like the previous example of someone lying to you but insisting they are telling the truth). Allow yourself to feel the emotions that come to you when thinking about this issue. You might feel tense, angry, sad, etc. Don't fight these feelings or even try to understand them, as this is getting into the realm of using reason. Just let them wash over you.

Now listen to that voice telling you what the truth is—not what you wish it to be and not what someone else has told you about it. Trust that your intuition is on the right track.

This is a skill that needs to be practiced and honed, especially if you've ignored your perceptions for some time. Some people have trouble determining what they feel about a situation when they start this process, but keep at it—intuition is like riding a bike. It will come back to you if you let it!

Psychic Skills

The stronger your intuition is, the more likely you are to develop other psychic abilities, such as one of the following.

Clairalience

Psychic information relayed by scent is clairalience. This is different than a memory being sparked by a smell—we all have a strong connection to certain scents from childhood or strong emotional experiences. Clairalience involves more of a "phantom" scent—something that only the intended recipient can detect. For example, some people experiencing hauntings will say they smell something putrid or, conversely, that they smell perfume or something similarly singular to a nearby spirit.

Clairaudience

Clairaudience is the ability to hear psychic communications, though it's not like hearing a low vibration or a high-pitched dog whistle. We're talking about hearing from relatives who have passed, or being aware of spiritual voices. Some of the voices may not make sense without more information. Why are you hearing an old woman's voice whenever your friend Mary is visiting? It could be her grandmother who recently passed away.

Clairsentience

Absorbing and experiencing the emotions surrounding you comprises clairsentience. People who have this ability are known as empaths, and they must learn to protect their spiritual space, as it is very easy to become inundated by pain, fear, anxiety, or other negative emotions. Empaths end up owning everyone else's emotional experiences, for better or worse!

Clairvoyance

This is the ability to see energies, events, or entities that aren't visible to most people. Mediums often experience clairvoyance when the spirits of those who have passed on appear during a divination, or when they can envision something that happened to you in the past—or something that is going to happen in the future.

Precognition

This involves having knowledge of an incident before it happens, whether through a vision or a dream. This is a little different from a premonition, which is the feeling that something good or bad is about to happen. A precognitive soul is someone who says, "Don't get on that train—it's going to derail!" Premonition is more like "I have an uneasy feeling about your upcoming trip."

Telepathy

Telepathy is communicating or sharing visions or feelings with someone without speaking. This is not the same as catching your best friend's eye in a crowded setting and knowing that you're both amused by the same thing. Telepathy is *knowing* that your brother is distressed, even though you live across the country and haven't spoken to him in a while.

Like intuition, psychic powers are something many of us are born with, but we learn to dismiss them during our formative years. This is a shame, of course, because we lose our connection to an entire universe filled with so much information. Think about how happy we would all be if we were completely confident in our thoughts and actions.

The good news is that there are many ways to regain your innate psychic abilities. One of the best methods is to use a crystal grid.

CRYSTAL GRIDS

The use of specific crystal layouts dates back thousands of years. Many of the shapes used are based on sacred geometry, which is what Stonehenge and the pyramids are also believed to have been based on. These layouts are used to enhance the power of the stones and can be used for a variety of reasons—not just for psychic skills. Some grids work by having crystals placed on the body, while others require having stones placed around a workspace. When used together in this manner, the stones resonate with one another and connect on a spiritual plane! You can change the vibration of a grid by adjusting the arrangement of the crystals.

This opens different energy fields and allows your own energy to be magnified.

Before forming any crystal grid, no matter the shape, be sure to thoroughly cleanse and empower your crystals (see chapter 2, pages 29–35). You should focus on your intention or question during the empowerment process.

Then, take a transparent crystal, such as clear quartz, and trace the outline of the grid around the crystals. This connects the energies of the stones to one another and activates them to work as a unit.

Crystals for Your Crown

To open your mind and boost your inner vision, you can use a simple grid called a crystal crown. For the sake of this introductory exercise, we'll choose amethyst, iolite, and clear quartz, which are malleable and work well both for protection and to enhance energetic combinations. We'll also need obsidian or black tourmaline.

Prepare a serene environment for yourself. Light some candles, burn incense, or use lavender (for relaxing) or peppermint (for energy) essential oils. Cleanse and empower your crystals (see chapter 2, pages 29–35), focusing on the question or issue around which you seek clarity. Breathe deeply while clearing all other thoughts.

Lie down on the bed and place the amethyst and iolite crystals next to each of your ears. Place the clear quartz on your forehead. In using this grid, you are balancing the hemispheres of your mind and allowing the crystal quartz to stabilize those energies.

You can also choose several other stones that will complement one another in this grid, such as desert rose agate (for intuition and mental calm) or Apache tears agate (for grounding, spiritual protection, and spiritual restoration) and place the entire group in a semicircle around your head.

To fully ground yourself, you should also place a black tourmaline or obsidian between your feet. This stone roots you to this world and keeps you safe during your mystical journey.

Direct your question to the universe and allow the answer to come to you in visions. You may see things that you don't understand at first, and that's all right. Allow every image to come and go without judgment or objection.

Give yourself a good ten to twenty minutes for this process. When the visions cease, write down what you observed in your mind's eye. Again, some of the images may not make sense immediately, but in the coming days, they may take on new meaning!

Circles and Ovals

Circular or oval grids are very basic, simple grids to put together, but they are more dynamic than square or rectangular grids, as there is no beginning or end to the shape. Energy is free to flow and is not in danger of slowing or getting stuck in a corner. These grids can be large or small, depending on whether you plan to sit or lie down in the circle.

For the circular grid, you don't need to have scores of stones to make a complete circle—just enough to form the basic shape. Cleanse and empower your crystals (see chapter 2, pages 29–35), focusing on your intention as you do so. Place your crystals on the floor or on your bed in the desired shape. Once you've put your crystals down, step back to make sure you're happy with the grid and the order of the stones. This is your psychic force field, after all, and it needs to meet your standards!

An oval grid should consist of approximately six quartz crystals that are relatively large. Place the quartz in the following positions, which align with the chakras:

- **One above your head**
- **One below your feet**
- **One at either side of the hips**
- **One at either side of the arms**

Lie in the oval's center and focus on the issue you're seeking clarity around. Have an open mind and heart in which to receive the answers.

Spirals and Stars

You can get creative with your grids and layouts—create a spiral or a star shape, or a rainbow or infinity shape. These shapes can be formed on a tabletop, as it may be difficult to place yourself in their centers.

Follow the same ritual as with any grid—cleanse and charge the stones prior to use (see chapter 2, pages 29–35), and then place your stones with intention, giving gratitude to each one.

In the case of a tabletop grid, you can write your intention and place it in the stone formation's center. You can place lit candles or other objects that hold special meaning to you into the layout as well. Tabletop grids can be left in place for as long as you like. Take care to visit the layout and focus on your intention daily.

Dream a Crystal Dream

For an easy psychic-enhancing grid, put your crystals underneath your pillow, or, if this will cause you to have a restless night, place them under your bed. Take care to cleanse and charge them first (see chapter 2, pages 29–35). Prepare yourself for bed prior to putting your crystals in place for the night.

Take a relaxing shower, all the while contemplating that the stones' energy will work while you sleep, and be open to the answers or visions that will come to you.

If you choose to place the crystals under your bed, don't just toss them underneath and hope for the best. Place them very deliberately, with thoughtfulness, directly under where you will be snoozing. Thank each stone as you place it for the work it will be doing for you.

Likewise, if the crystals are going under your pillow, give gratitude for each stone. Turn out the lights, relax, breathe deeply, and let the answers come to you in your sleep.

A Crystal Grid Spell for All-Seeing

Using a crystal grid is a great way to consolidate and boost an energetic field. You can use this energy for a lot of things—healing, mediation, cleansing, and, of course, psychic vision. Now that you know about arranging your crystals for maximum energy flow, let's talk about a special ritual that will work in conjunction with your precious stones to amplify and expand your psychic abilities.

Practitioners of magick know that spells are used only for positive intentions and that whatever you project to the universe, you will go on to receive once the affirmation returns to you. This spell for all-seeing is a magickal ritual that requires a bit of time and commitment.

Materials

Your crystal grid, using crystals of your choosing
(see list on top of page 92 for inspiration)

Epsom salts

Several votive or tealight candles, in white

A crystal wand, using kyanite or clear quartz

A separate piece of crystal, of your choosing

Ritual

Cleanse and empower your crystals (see chapter 2, pages 29–35), and then form your crystal grid in the shape of your choice. Begin by setting your intention. Sit quietly and say to yourself, "I am performing this ritual so that I can see what is unseen." If there is a specific issue you want to know about, say something like "I want to see the person I will spend my life with."

Now prepare a cleansing bath with the Epsom salts, continuing to mediate on your intention all the while. This is a means of clearing your mind and cleansing any preconceived notions. Focus on purity of the mind during this time. Soak in the tub for at least twenty minutes, then rinse your body with clean water from the shower or spigot. Dry yourself with a clean towel.

Your spell-casting site can be set up indoors or outdoors, whichever is more comfortable and fills you with more inspiration. Light the candles, which will help to clear away any cluttered energy.

Hold the crystal wand in your dominant hand and the crystal of your choosing in the other hand. Point the wand at your grid and trace a line from one crystal to the next, activating the energy in the layout. Close your eyes and breathe deeply, again focusing on purity of vision and sharing in the crystals' energy.

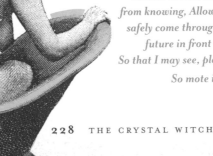

Now recite the following spell (or create an incantation using your own words):

"Crystal power, strengthen my vision,
So that I may know what is right and true.

Loosen the ties that prevent me
from knowing, Allow the messages to
safely come through. Show me my
future in front of my eyes,
So that I may see, please be my guide.
So mote it be."

Thank the crystals for their assistance and let the crystal grid sit undisturbed. You can place the wand inside of the stone formation if you like. The spell is likely to manifest over the next few days, so during this time, try to pay attention to any visions that might come to you.

For even more powerful results, try practicing this spell outside under the light of a full moon.

Crystal Pyramids

You can also use a crystal pyramid to help develop your psychic abilities. A crystal pyramid is simply a crystal or stone that has been carved into the form of a pyramid. Smaller versions are quite affordable, depending on the variety of stone used, whereas larger pyramids can be higher in price. While crystal pyramids are not technically grids, the shape itself draws in and organizes spiritual energy so that you can access it in a focused form. You can use a large or small crystal pyramid for our purposes. Smaller stones can be held in your hands, while larger version can be used as a focal point.

If you are holding a small pyramid in your hands, close your eyes and focus on clearing your mind, which allows your psychic skills to expand. If you're using a large pyramid, soften your gaze while looking at the stone and allow the wisdom and knowledge you're seeking to come to you.

WEARING CRYSTALS

An easy way to keep your psychic-boosting crystals nearby at all times is by wearing them. Not only will you sparkle and shine; you'll be able to easily draw upon whatever energy you need at that time. You can include magickal stones in any form of wearable accessory, such as bracelets, necklaces, earrings, rings, hair pieces, brooches, or belts.

Many diviners wear jewelry that contains a protective stone, as they are never sure what kind of forces they'll meet in a psychic session. Some of the best protective stones for this purpose are:

- **Black tourmaline**
- **Fluorite**
- **Hematite**
- **Kyanite**
- **Onyx**
- **Pyrite**

You can find crystal wearables of every style in New Age shops and any number of retailers, or you can craft your own.

Crystal Sleep Mask

It's possible for your dreams to become disturbed after a psychic session. Sometimes you just can't shake energies loose right away, and they show up as vivid images in your sleep. If this happens, you can place a protective stone under your bed or pillow, or you can incorporate small pieces of a protective crystal into an eye mask to wear overnight.

Materials

- A store-bought sleep mask with an elastic band
- Fabric glue
- A small piece of protective crystal

Ritual

Cleanse and empower your crystal (see chapter 2, pages 29–35), envisioning peaceful, undisturbed sleep as you do so. When ready, simply glue the crystal piece to your eye mask. It should be placed right around where your Third Eye Chakra is—in the middle of your brow.

Wear this protective headgear when you go to sleep for as long as it takes your strange dreams to resolve.

CRYSTALS FOR THE ZODIAC

There's something very interesting about astrological signs—they tend to be spot-on in describing the energy of the people born under a specific alignment of the cosmos. Each sign has a set of crystals that can help a person connect with psychic energy during any sort of divination session. We've talked about crystal grids, crystals with tasseomancy, tarot cards clarified by crystals, and how to add crystals to other fortune-telling techniques. This section will give you specific guidance about more crystals you may want to try based on your birthday.

Traditional Birthstones by Month

You are probably already aware of the gemstone that corresponds to the month you were born. Before we explore the zodiacal gemstones, here is the list of traditional stones by month:

JANUARY: Garnet

FEBRUARY: Amethyst

MARCH: Aquamarine or Bloodstone

APRIL: Diamond

MAY: Emerald

JUNE: Pearl, Alexandrite, or Moonstone

JULY: Ruby

AUGUST: Peridot or Spinel

SEPTEMBER: Sapphire

OCTOBER: Opal or Tourmaline

NOVEMBER: Topaz or Citrine

DECEMBER: Tanzanite, Zircon, or Turquoise

ARIES

(MARCH 21—APRIL 19)

Sign of the Ram

· RUBY ·

ALSO: ALEXANDRITE · CARNELIAN
· CITRINE · DIAMOND · FIRE AGATE
· GARNET · FLUORITE

Aries are a friendly sort, but they do love a good competition. In fact, these folks need to feel challenged all the time in order to be at their best. Aries love to have a lot of irons in the fire. They are fiercely loyal and protective of the ones they love and thrive on a structured schedule. They have very strong ideas about how life should be and will not stop working until their visions become a reality.

Some Aries come off as pressured, but it's really their high energy level that makes them seem as though they're bursting at the seams. They aren't afraid to be confrontational, but they are also the first to pitch in, lend a hand, and tell someone they're doing a great job.

TAURUS

(APRIL 20—MAY 20)

Sign of the Bull

· TOPAZ ·

ALSO: LEXANDRITE · AMBLYGONITE
· CARNELIAN · EMERALD · GARNET · MALACHITE
· OBSIDIAN · PERIDOT · QUARTZ

Taureans sometimes get a bad rap as being stubborn and disagreeable, but this isn't necessarily the case. While it's true that Taureans can be like a dog with a bone when they find something they're interested in, they're likely to want to share that passion with other people. Like Aries, the Taurus is a hard worker and can't stand to leave a job unfinished.

Honesty is everything to the Taurus, so don't try to pull the wool over their eyes. They're sharp and can sense when someone is lying to them. They are absolutely driven in every area of their life and can't rest until all the pieces of a relationship or project are falling into place.

GEMINI

(MAY 21—JUNE 20)

Sign of the Twins

• TOURMALINE •

ALSO: AQUAMARINE • CHALCEDONY • CLEAR QUARTZ
• DIAMOND • LABRADORITE • MOONSTONE
• OBSIDIAN • OPAL • TURQUOISE

The Gemini is one of the dual personalities of the zodiac. They are adept at blending into any situation with any group, making fast friends and becoming the center of attention. They are witty, creative, and full of energy. They tend to have lots of friends and feed off the energy of others. Geminis are the people who call you at midnight with a crazy idea and end the call by saying, "Get dressed! I'll be there in five minutes!"

Geminis are loud, boisterous, inappropriate at times, and always up for as much fun as possible. Still, as much as this star sign loves life, they can also be hit hard by the blues. The good news is that they are eternal optimists and will always pull themselves up out of the doldrums. Divination surrounding creativity is a great exercise for Geminis.

CANCER

(JUNE 21—JULY 22)
Sign of the Crab

· MOONSTONE ·

ALSO: AVENTURINE · BLACK TOURMALINE
· CHALCEDONY · EMERALD · JADE
· SELENITE · QUARTZ

Cancer is one of the gentlest souls in the zodiac. Creative, intuitive, and nurturing, these folks are extremely loyal to their loved ones. This sign is driven to connect with a higher power of some sort, whether it's nature, God, or their own art. Inspiration is the cornerstone of their happiness, and without it, Cancer gets restless.

These folks rely heavily on their feelings to determine the truth of a situation. This is a good thing if you have a Cancer in your corner—it's not such a great thing if you are a Cancer and you're starting to lose sight of the truth. Their empathic nature can become a heavy load to bear at times, and Cancers need time on their own to recharge.

LEO

(JULY 23—AUGUST 22)

Sign of the Lion

• TIGER'S EYE •

ALSO: ALEXANDRITE • CHRYSOBERYL
• CITRINE • GOLDEN TOPAZ • MALACHITE
• PERIDOT • RUBY

Who loves to have all eyes on them and makes no bones about it? Leo, of course! A Leo is like a more forceful and focused version of Gemini, always having a plan and working hard to make it come to fruition. A Leo is someone who knows not only what they need to do—they know what *you* need to do, too, and want you to hop to it! This sign has boundless energy and high standards. They want the best in every situation and will make sure they get it.

The lion is a perfect symbol of Leo's courage and dominant personality. Don't think they're arrogant by nature; these people are just consumed by the desire to have and do it all.

VIRGO

(AUGUST 23—SEPTEMBER 22)

Sign of the Virgin

• OPAL •

ALSO: AMETHYST • BLUE CALCITE
• CARNELIAN • AGATE • IOLITE • MOONSTONE
• OBSIDIAN • PINK TOPAZ • SAPPHIRE

Sweet, sweet Virgo. They are the givers of the zodiac, always kind, always willing to listen to a sad story or lend a hand to a friend in need of help. These traits are coupled with an artistic flair and the ability to see the potential in people, places, and situations that may seem rather ordinary at first glance. Virgos' sensitive souls are often expressed in a quiet nature, but as the saying goes, still waters run deep. Virgos have a rich imaginative life and are never bored by their own company.

Virgos expect a lot from themselves. This is obvious in the way they dress, the way they keep house, and the company in which they surround themselves. Their tight circle of friends is reserved for those they know and trust beyond the shadow of a doubt. If you have a Virgo as a close friend, they will never let you down!

LIBRA

(SEPTEMBER 23—OCTOBER 22)

Sign of the Scales

· EMERALD ·

ALSO: AVENTURINE · CAT'S-EYE · CLEAR QUARTZ
· HELIOTROPE · PINK TOURMALINE
· RAINBOW FLUORITE · PERIDOT · SAPPHIRE

Justice is the name of the game for Libras. These folks are concerned with keeping things fair and square and are especially good at coming up with creative compromises during tense situations. Libras have big-picture visions and can see and sense multiple outcomes for any given set of circumstances.

Libras are one part imagination and one part practicality, which makes them grounded dreamers. They tend to mull over deep questions, like the purpose of life, all the while willing to dig in and do whatever it takes to make themselves and others happy.

SCORPIO

(OCTOBER 23—NOVEMBER 21)
Sign of the Scorpion

• RUBY •

ALSO: ALEXANDRITE • CARNELIAN • DIAMOND
• HEMATITE • OBSIDIAN • OPAL • PINK TOURMALINE
• SNOWFLAKE • OBSIDIAN • TOPAZ

One of the boldest signs of the zodiac, Scorpios mean business and aren't afraid to let you know it! This sign can come off as bold, intimidating, arrogant, and fearless, but they most often have a heart of gold to back it all up. Being a Scorpio is all about being real. They know what they want, and they are very clear about this in all areas of their life.

Beneath what can seem like a rough exterior lies a fiercely loyal nature. Scorpios are very in tune with their emotions and will go to the ends of the earth to protect the ones they love. They have a real zest for life and don't give up on anything or anyone.

SAGITTARIUS

(NOVEMBER 22—DECEMBER 21)
Sign of the Archer

• TOPAZ •

ALSO: AMETHYST • BLACK TOURMALINE • BLUE
CHALCEDONY • CALCITE • LAPIS LAZULI • RUBY
• SMOKY QUARTZ • SODALITE • TURQUOISE

Sagittarius is the model student, employee, and friend. Truthful, generous, and caring, these folks go above and beyond for those they care about. They tend not to mince words, although they are diplomatic and soft-spoken. They are also very intelligent and seek to grow and learn at every stage of life.

Above all else, a Sagittarius is a trusting and trustworthy soul. This is the person to whom you can tell your deepest thoughts and secrets, and you can not only trust them to keep your confidence but to give you good advice as well!

CAPRICORN

(DECEMBER 22—JANUARY 19)
Sign of the Goat

• GARNET •

ALSO: AMETHYST • BLACK TOURMALINE • BLUE
CHALCEDONY • CALCITE CHRYSOBERYL • DIAMOND
• EMERALD • MALACHITE• OBSIDIAN • TURQUOISE

This sign loves order, rules, and planned activities. However, they have a great sense of humor and tend to do well with all personality types. These are people who know and genuinely like everyone they meet and make friends out of strangers almost instantly. Capricorns give everyone the benefit of the doubt, but don't cross them—they also have a stubborn streak a mile wide and are slow to forgive serious transgressions.

Capricorns are persistent people and pursue their goals with enthusiasm. They tend to have an eye for detail and enjoy work that others might find tedious or dull.

AQUARIUS

(JANUARY 20—FEBRUARY 18)
Sign of the Water Bearer

• TOPAZ AND SAPPHIRE •

ALSO: AMETHYST • AQUAMARINE • GARNET
• LABRADORITE • MOONSTONE •
• RUTILATED QUARTZ •

Like Geminis, Aquarians tend to have a dual nature: one part of them is outgoing, gregarious, and full of energy, whereas the other side is quiet, contemplative, and creative. These folks are intuition grounded in logic, and if this sounds confusing to you . . . well, Aquarians will tell you that it is, indeed, perplexing at times!

Because Aquarians need time alone to recharge, they can come off as aloof. The truth is that they often crave connection but are just too exhausted by the energies of others to engage one-on-one.

PISCES

(FEBRUARY 19—MARCH 20)
Sign of the Fish

• AMETHYST AND ONYX •

ALSO: AQUAMARINE • BLOODSTONE
• FLUORITE • LABRADORITE • LAPIS LAZULI
• MOONSTONE • TURQUOISE

Pisceans are the dreamers of the zodiac. They tend to be kind, generous, nurturing souls who appear to have their heads in the clouds all the time. They often forget to show up on time or do the things they said they would, but there's never any malice involved. Pisces just get lost in their daydreams!

These folks struggle with schedules, order, and authority. They simply want to be free to create, meditate, and love the people in their circle. They are very open to psychic energy and are often empathic.

Chapter 8

Reiki for Well-being

THERE ARE AS MANY WAYS TO USE YOUR CRYSTALS AS there are crystals themselves. Healing rituals are especially popular, as they allow you to connect physically and spiritually during a single session. In this chapter, we'll cover the healing practice of Reiki and how to incorporate crystals into a session, as well as less structured ways to use your crystals for better health of the mind, body, and soul.

The following crystals are suggestions. Feel free to use a crystal that you feel best matches your specific needs when it comes to healing rituals. Refer to the A–Z Guide and reference guides in chapter 4 for more information.

WHAT IS REIKI?

Each of us has a life force flowing through our bodies. This is the essence of who we are, something separate from the physical body. Some cultures refer to this as *qi*, *chi*, *ki*, or *prana*. Sometimes the flow of energy gets stuck or runs low. Fortunately, there are several practices that can rev up that energy and get it moving in the right direction.

Reiki, one such practice, is believed to have been founded in 1920s Japan by Mikao Usui, a spiritual leader who sought to connect his students with the universal life force. (In Japanese, *rei* means "universal life" and *ki* means "energy.") Usui's goal was to provide men and women with a spiritual base that would aid in their self-esteem and development.

The purpose of a Reiki session can be multifold. It can focus on physical healing, spiritual development, or relaxation, or all three. Reiki rests on the idea that all healing starts with the self and that the stronger the self is, the more likely you are to find yourself on the road to recovery! Of course, you should always follow your doctor's advice concerning a physical diagnosis and treatment, but at the very least, Reiki can promote a sense of calm and well-being that allows you to focus on your recuperation. Reiki is also a totally noninvasive practice, so there's nothing to lose—and the universe to gain!

GET READY TO REIKI

Because true Reiki training takes a long time, we're going to discuss the highlights and focus on self-healing with crystals. For a more complete picture of how to provide a Reiki healing session for someone else, you can download a chart of Reiki hand positions for use with clients. As this practice has grown in popularity, some communities have begun offering classes at public libraries or through continuing education courses. Keep an eye out for these opportunities if you're interested in a hands-on training experience!

Signs You Could Benefit from a Reiki Session

- Confusion or lack of direction on an issue
- Ongoing stress
- You're undergoing a major life change that has yet to resolve itself
- Chronic physical issues

Setting up your Reiki work area is simple. First, find a quiet, serene spot, indoors or out. You know what to do—light a candle, burn some incense or fire up your essential oil diffuser, and turn on relaxing sounds or music. Practice deep breathing while you prepare your workspace. Put all your love and intention toward creating a healing environment for yourself.

Now lie down or sit, making sure you're completely at ease. Continue your deep breathing. Starting with your toes, contract and release your muscles and limbs in isolated groups (for example, wiggle your toes, then relax; roll your ankles, then relax; flex your calves, then relax; etc.). Work your way up to your head, where you can purse your lips, smile broadly, scrunch your nose, blink your eyes . . . and then relax those muscles.

What did you observe during that body scan?

- Did you feel pain anywhere?

- How about general discomfort (tightness in the shoulders or neck, for example)?

- Is there lingering tension? Can you breathe into those areas to relax them?

- If there are physical areas of your body that need healing, how do you feel about it? Are you angry? Frustrated? Sad?

- What are your feelings related to being unable to control everything in your body?

The purpose of this scan is to identify both physical and spiritual areas for healing. Tension can manifest as a physical issue (like tight shoulders or a headache), but it originates with a stressful trigger.

Hopefully you now you have a pretty good idea of what spiritual and physical areas need a little attention.

Reiki Hands

Healing from Reiki comes through your hands. There are fifteen hand positions:

1. Hands over your face, fingertips toward the top of the forehead and your palms extending down toward your chin. The sides of your palms should touch.

2. Hands cup ears.

3. Hands horizontal at the back of your head, one high, one low.

4. Right hand on your throat; left hand over your heart.

5. Hands cup the neck on either side.

6. Hands on your upper abdomen, fingertips touching.

7. Hands on your mid-abdomen, fingertips touching.

8. Hands on your lower abdomen, fingertips touching.

9. Hands on the lower back above the hip bones, fingertips touching.

10. Hands on the lower back at the sacrum, fingertips touching.

11. Hands hold the left foot.

12. Hands hold the right foot.

13. Left hand holds left foot; right hand holds right foot.

14. Left hand holds right foot; right hand holds left foot.

15. Cup the right hand over the top of the head in the center, left hand touching in the middle of the lower back.

Some Reiki experts advise holding each hand position for about three minutes. Others say that you should let the flow of energy and intuition guide your hands, and if an area needs more time, you can allow your hands to linger. You will get a sense for what feels right as you practice more.

These are the best crystals to add to your Reiki practice for optimum energy flow:

AMETHYST Helps neutralize negative energy

BLACK TOURMALINE Good for grounding, protection from dark energies, and neutralizing negative energy

CLEAR QUARTZ Strengthens the immune system and promotes healing; brings balance to the bodily systems

ROSE QUARTZ Promotes love, calm, self-esteem, and self-forgiveness

SELENITE Brings protection to a meditative session, along with calming energy and mental clarity

Choose your crystals according to your specific needs and situate them around your work area on tables or shelves in the room. Additionally, you can rest a crystal on or next to the area that needs extra healing. Keep a Reiki journal to note which crystals match best with your practice.

THE POWER OF CRYSTAL TOUCH

If Reiki seems too complicated for you, you can still use a simplified version of crystal healing to boost the flow of good energy and help rid your mind and body of negative energy. Create your own ritual using your instinct and connection to your spirit. There are many crystals that have specific spiritual and emotional benefits, although their effectiveness does depend on whether you are the type of person that responds well to crystal energy. Here are some key crystals that you can use to direct positive energy to certain areas and issues:

AGATE Brain function and communication

CITRINE Digestion; mental sharpness

FLUORITE Inflammation and mental sharpness

HEMATITE Circulatory system and anxiety

JADE Joint pain

KYANITE Headaches and tension

LAPIS LAZULI Throat, voice, and neck

MOONSTONE Digestive issues, weight gain, hormones

OPAL Eyes

TURQUOISE Head—neck, ears, and brain

Whether you are healing yourself or a loved one, choose a crystal according to your need. You can place it over the affected area or create a crystal grid (see pages 222–29) with several crystals and place yourself or your loved one inside of the layout. As noted earlier, while you can use crystals for help with certain ailments, they are not a replacement for modern medicine and should not be relied upon to cure illnesses or health issues. Please consult with your doctor as needed.

If you are using crystals in your own healing, allow at least twenty minutes for your session. Lie down or sit quietly with the crystals in place and visualize the affected area rejuvenating itself. Imagine yourself back to perfect health. Feel the crystal energy as it encompasses the area in question and surrounds it with a gentle, loving force field. Know that you are supported in your healing by these stones. If you are assisting someone in their healing, gently guide the session by reminding them of these visualizations. Allow the person quiet time to open themselves to the positive energy.

CRYSTALS TO SOOTHE THE SOUL

The same crystals used to help with physical ailments have spiritual healing properties as well. Using the same type of ritual and placing the crystals either on the body or in a grid, you can create a mindful healing zone.

AGATE Negates negative energy and promotes healing around issues of self-esteem, anger, and doubt

AMAZONITE Grounds and helps heal emotional trauma

CITRINE Relates to money and improving financial situations

FLUORITE Protects from negative energy and boosts positive intention

HEMATITE A grounding stone; helps keep its user rooted in the moment

JADE Opens the heart and allows its holder to see and accept a situation for what it is

KYANITE Increases connection to the universe; great for meditation; healing and protective for those experiencing loss

LAPIS LAZULI Opens its user to creative thought and expression, especially when ideas are not being heard or appreciated

MOONSTONE Helps mend an out-of-control ego

OPAL A conduit to the psychic realm; opens the Third Eye Chakra for better understanding

TURQUOISE Protects its user, supports communication, and promotes intuition

Let's say that you work in an office where your ideas are seldom heard and you're worried that, because of this, you're going to be seen as a lackluster employee. Try remedying this with lapis lazuli in combination with citrine. Perform your own meditation first, then keep these stones with you during your next meeting or on your desk. You may find you have new energy to draw from, energy that helps you persist and get your point across.

Or, if you are struggling to get over the breakup of a relationship, you might like to carry a piece of jade in your pocket or wear it as jewelry.

This should hopefully settle down your emotions and leave you feeling more accepting of the situation.

Whatever your need, carrying, wearing or sleeping with the correct corresponding stone could leave you feeling more empowered and ready to face another day.

Chapter 9

Connect with Your Spirit

THROUGHOUT THIS BOOK, WE HAVE DISCUSSED MANY ways to put your crystals to use. Meditation is an important part of connecting with your higher self and is very helpful when calling on your spirit guides for assistance. In this section, we'll look at how to get yourself into a meditative state using crystals, to open your mind and find your truest self.

Many people shrug off the idea of meditation, believing they can't relax long enough to get into an ethereal state of mind. The good news is that there are many forms of meditation, and if the traditional form doesn't appeal to you, then perhaps there's another way to get you connected to the universal flow.

MINDFUL MEDITATIONS
WITH CRYSTALS

To perform a meditation at home, you should first choose a space that is comfortable, quiet, and free from distraction (although the point is to eventually master your mind enough that nothing can distract you). For initial sessions, set aside just several minutes for meditation; this should be enough time to give you an idea of what it's like to remove all emotional debris and just be in the moment.

Choose a crystal or two, based on the issues you want to focus on (see chapter 5 for inspiration). For example, if you are experiencing fallout from some type of emotional trauma, holding amazonite can promote a sense of well-being and safety. Alternatively, create a crystal grid (see pages 222–29).

Light a candle or stick of incense. If you have an essential oil diffuser, add a few drops of lavender.

Sit or lie down comfortably and close your eyes. Now start breathing as deeply as possible. You may want to count to eight while you inhale, then do it again as you exhale. Scan your body during this time, from your toes to your forehead, to relax any areas of tension. Pay special attention to the crystals in your hands or situated around you. Can you feel the vibrations radiating off them? Is the energy warm? Relaxing? Invigorating?

When you feel completely relaxed, let your mind open only to the present and whatever the issue is around which you seek clarity. For example, if you're suffering from emotional trauma, try not to think about the past or the feelings that live there. Allow yourself to be only in *this* moment. Remind yourself that you are safe right here, right now. No matter what stress exists in your life, the point of meditation is to know that the present moment is all there ever is. The past is gone; the future is uncertain. Understanding this helps to eliminate anxiety and depression surrounding any issue.

Mantra Meditation

If other thoughts creep in (and they will, because we're human), set them aside for now. There will be time to think about them later if you so choose. If you have a hard time keeping your mind from wandering, you can repeat a word or phrase over and over in your mind to refocus. Your mantra could be a statement or request, like "I am safe," "Help me to see," or "Open my mind to true knowing," or it could be as simple as a word. There are many ancient mantras to choose from if you're not sure what to say. One of the most popular is the sacred Sanskrit syllable "om," a sound that in many Eastern religions is a mystical embodiment of the universe. Another mantra is the Sanskit "So 'ham," meaning "I am he/she/that." These mantras are grounding, reminding us that we can only be ourselves. You can create your own mantras for meditation. Just keep it simple and have it relate to your current needs.

Moving Meditation

If you're the type of person who just can't sit still, experts would probably suggest that meditation is *especially* good for you! But if you just can't get into it, you can learn to meditate while moving as well.

Using the same principles as before (without closing your eyes, of course), take your crystals on a walk, preferably through a park or other peaceful setting. Breathe deeply, focusing on using your senses and being mindful of your surroundings—take note of what you see, hear, and smell, and of how each of these observations makes you feel. Notice the weight of your crystals in your hand or on your person. The point of a mindful walk is to keep yourself grounded in the moment. This can be very helpful for those who aren't able to sit quietly without intrusive thoughts.

CONNECTING WITH SPIRIT GUIDES USING CRYSTALS

You can use meditation to connect with ancient gods and goddesses, too. These spirit guides can help you find your purpose and lead you along the path of enlightenment related to your questions and concerns.

Consider the following Greek gods and goddesses sources of information and knowledge:

APHRODITE Goddess of beauty and love; rules over issues of romance; a good source to call upon when searching for or confused in love

ARTEMIS Goddess of the hunt; assists with modern-day searching for work, homes, love, and the like

ATHENA Protector goddess; promotes safety and well-being; a great go-to when feeling unsure or anxious; calms the soul

ATLAS Titan of the burden; tasked with bearing the world on his shoulders; a kindred spirit for those feeling overwhelmed

GAIA Earth goddess, goddess of creation and conception; a good spirit to assist with creative endeavors or matters of the home

HERA Goddess of domestic affairs, rules over issues of the home; seek her assistance in matters of children, marriage, or moving

HYPERION Titan of light and embodiment of ethereal light; a positive energy and protective deity

POSEIDON Ruler of the seas and all bodies of water; as water is a calming force, Poseidon can help soothe worries; gives great strength, as water is a powerful force

PROMETHEUS Creator of humans, ruler of mankind; helps with personal issues and gaining greater understanding

URANUS The sky god, a great prophet; may assist with psychic vision and clarity

ZEUS King of the Greek gods, ruler of ethereal bodies; assists with connecting to other spirits and knowing the godliness within yourself

To connect with the gods and goddesses during meditation, hold a crystal of your choosing (align your choice with your intent, or choose a crystal that you've worked with in the past and had good results with) and invoke them with a simple request. For instance, to summon Athena, you could say:

> *"Athena, I ask that you come to me,*
> *work through me, help me to know I am protected*
> *and safe throughout my meditation."*

Continue with your meditation, using a mantra if you find it helpful and opening to whatever comes to you.

ANGEL MEDITATIONS

Because they act as an immediate connection between this realm and the heavens, many people want to hear from angels or speak with a specific angel. Some folks already know the name of their angel—like

Raphael, Michael, or Gabriel, who are three of the archangels. Others know they always have a protective force nearby—a guardian angel—and want to know their name. A crystal meditation can provide these answers with the fluttering of a wing.

Angel meditations generally focus on giving thanks, asking for protection or assistance for oneself or for loved ones, or asking for guidance. Choose from one of the following crystals to connect with your angel guide:

ANGELITE What stone could be more perfect for this meditation? This clear crystal helps channel and clarify information and guidance from angels.

ANGEL PHANTOM QUARTZ This stone is known to strengthen one's connection to the angelic realm.

AQUAMARINE This crystal helps purify the mind and make hearing the messages from angelic guides easier.

CELESTITE (CELESTINE) Another stone that's perfectly in tune with the celestial realms, celestite is a crystal associated with divine timing.

CLEAR QUARTZ This is another purifying stone that enables one to open the mind to divine messages.

ROSE QUARTZ Known for its healing vibrations, rose quartz opens its holder to the loving energy of angels.

Follow the same guidelines as you would for a regular meditation, holding a crystal in each hand (or have them in a crystal grid) while opening your mind to divine messages. For connection to the heavens throughout the day, try wearing one or more of these stones in the form of jewelry.

Chapter 10

Crystals through the Year

THERE IS NO BETTER WAY TO MARK SPECIAL DATES IN the calendar than with an endless variety of annual festivities. Over the years and with each religion, celebrations have evolved to suit the current faith and culture. (It is common knowledge that many Christian holidays are derived from an ancient pagan faith, for instance—Easter is a perfect example.) Wiccans, however, are more inclined to follow traditional customs to the letter. This chapter examines some of the origins of these special dates and shows you the spells, rituals, and symbolic items (including crystals) witches use to commemorate significant dates today.

While the following pages encapsulate a general overview of significant Wiccan dates, the history and traditions, deities worshiped, and rituals performed do vary from culture to culture.

YULE

(WINTER SOLSTICE) | DECEMBER 20—23

Yule initially began with the earliest winter solstice festivals, in pre-Christian Northern Europe. Yuletide, as we know it today, represented the first day of winter. The Feast of Juul was celebrated by the ancient Germanic people and lasted twelve days, during which time they would grieve the death of the old god and honor the goddess while she gave birth to the new Sun King. In commemoration, they would burn a Yule or Juul log lit from a small part of the previous year's tree, to ensure good luck.

These traditions traveled around Europe: the French cut up the log and brought a small amount inside to burn each day. In Cornwall, England, the Cornish would remove all bark before burning. In some parts of the United Kingdom, they replaced the log with ash twigs or candles. Nowadays, we prefer to cover a Swiss roll cake in chocolate and delight in the pleasures of indulgence. In times gone by, people celebrated Yuletide by feasting and giving gifts of food to neighbors and friends. This may be where the tradition of gift-giving during Christmas was born.

THE YULE LOG

Yuletide Elements and Traditions

It is common practice to place shining objects on the altar, such as glitter, yellow candles, or sparkly, adorned ornaments. These signify the return of sun. Other ways you might like to celebrate are as follows:

- **BELLS** It is traditional to ring a small bell over the altar to cast out any demons that might surface during the darker days of winter.

- **CANDLES** Candles of red, green, or blue should be burned upon the altar through the twelve days of Yule. (Extinguish them each night and relight them each day.)

- **CRYSTALS** Alexandrite, black onyx, blue topaz, citrine, clear quartz, garnet, kunzite, lemon quartz, pearl, peridot, ruby, green tourmaline, snowflake obsidian, diamonds

- **DEITIES** Brigid, Green Man, Holly King, Oak King, Triple Goddess (Pagan/Celtic); Apollo, Artemis, Demeter, Gaia (Greek); Isis, Ra (Egyptian); Odin (Germanic/Norse); sun gods

- **EVERGREENS** Poinsettias, Christmas cactus, ivy

- **HERBS** Bay, blessed thistle, chamomile, cinnamon, evergreen, holly, frankincense, juniper, laurel, sage, yellow cedar

- **HOLLY** Wards off any evil spirits; bring it indoors to keep energies sweet

- **INCENSE** Bayberry, cedar, cinnamon, pine

- **MISTLETOE** Symbolizes fertility

- **TREES** Origin of indoor Christmas trees; originally, apples and pastries hung from the branches; cut branches throughout the home symbolize spring to come

- **WREATH** Symbolizes growth and everlasting life; can be worn as crowns, to celebrate fertility and the changing seasons; represents the wheel of the year when affixed to the center of altars

A Yuletide Spell

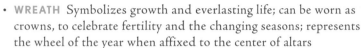

Spellwork during Yuletide should be performed with happiness and harmony in mind. Any intentions related to love, romance, and gratitude are sure to be successful. Witches love to cast spells at this time of year, showing thanks for the past twelve months and ensuring a safe and abundant winter in the months ahead.

Materials

A piece of crystal (see list on opposite page)

Items that represent Yule (see opposite page and above)

Celtic Christmas-themed music

Candles, in red, green, or gold

Wand (optional)

Small bell

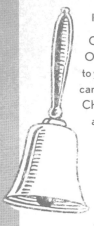

Cleanse and empower your crystal (see chapter 2, pages 29–35). On December 21, set up your altar with any items that represent Yule to you, along with the candles in the color(s) of your choice. Light the candles. Place the crystal on your altar, next to the candles. Play Celtic Christmas music; this is a must, as it will set the scene for a balanced and settled ritual.

If you have a wand, rotate it in a clockwise direction over your altar to cast a circle (alternatively, you can use your pointer finger). Next, ring the bell for a minute or two; this clears away unwanted energies left behind from the previous year and magickally sterilizes your workspace. Kneel (or sit on a chair) in front of your altar and speak the following yuletide incantation twelve times:

"Yule is upon us. I thank the gods for all the blessings bestowed upon me.
Keep me safe and free from harm as wintertime appears.
Blessed be."

After you've recited the spell twelve times, close it by adding *"So mote it be."* You can also create your own spell by writing yourself an ode to Yule. Remember, being a witch doesn't mean you have to follow set rules. Make it personal and go wherever the wind takes you!

IMBOLC

FEBRUARY 2

The soil is stirring, seeds are starting to sprout, and the cold, dark days of winter are at last in the past. The Old Irish word *imbolc* (pronounced *im-bulk* or *IM-bullug*) translates to "in the belly of the mother," meaning that, with the onset of spring, new life is expected. During this reawakening of the earth, Imbolc, which corresponds with the Christian holiday Candlemas, marks a crucial time within the wheel of the year for fertility and growth. This tradition honors Brigid, the triple pagan goddess of healing and the hearth. She generates fertility to the land and its individuals and is especially connected to birth. Spells and rituals for fertility and abundance are cast at this time, and this period inspires a thorough spring-clean, clearing away the old and making way for the new. Imbolc is also a fire pageant.

Imbolc Elements and Traditions

- **CANDLES** Yellow, pink, or white; wish spells should be performed for yourself, friends, and family. Simply light the candles, speak your wishes and needs aloud, close with *"So mote it be,"* and allow the candles to burn down.

- **CRYSTALS** Moonstone, rose quartz, jade

- **DEITIES** Brigid (Pagan/Celtic)

- **HERBS** Angelica, basil, bay, blackberry, heather, ginger, and violets

- **INCENSE** Basil, bay, cinnamon, myrrh, wisteria, vanilla

- **FLOWERS** Daffodil, iris, gorse, peony, violets, or any seasonal spring flowers

- **PLANTING SEEDS** February 1–2 are magickal days to plant seeds or flowers that will later bloom when the weather warms up. When you have finished planting your seeds in the ground, stand over the soil and make a silent wish for the coming season.

- **SPRING BAKE** Cakes baked with ingredients such as caraway and lemons; during the stirring of the mixture, an incantation is spoken repeatedly over the top of the cake: *"As I stir, good luck will grow; with this mixture, blessings will flow."* When cool, the cake is decorated with a large yellow ribbon and seasonal flowers.

- **SPRING POPPET** Many witches make a spring doll to represent the goddess Brigid from white, pink, red, or yellow fabric. This is usually done by folding a piece of material in half, marking out the doll's desired shape, and then cutting it out. The doll is then sewn and filled with seasonal herbs and/or dried flowers. One of the associated crystals should also be placed inside before the doll is stitched closed. Small children love to get involved with this exercise and delight in drawing in the faces or attaching wool to the head for hair.

  - **SWAN FEATHERS** Represent devotion, loyalty, and fidelity; can be used as charms and talismans to attract love and dependability

  - **TREES** Many witches with gardens have a rowan tree growing somewhere on their land. This tree magickally offers protection from all things evil. Use the bark or the leaves from a weeping willow to represent movement and change.

An Imbolc Spell

Spells for good luck, money, wealth, prosperity, and new beginnings are effective during Imbolc. A good-luck spell in particular is often executed on February 1–2, so it is important to present objects on your altar that represent spring.

Materials

Flowers, such as irises and daffodils

A vase

Candles, in yellow, pink, or white

Cake

Brigid poppet with a piece of crystal inside
(see list of crystals on page 267)

Ritual

Put the flowers in the vase and place them in the center of your workspace. The candles can be dotted around the outside of the vase. Have the cake and Brigid poppet nearby. The crystal should be inside your poppet, so make sure you have previously empowered the crystal with your needs. When you have your altar just how you like it, light the candles and say the following spell once:

"As the winter is now past, this wish I make at last,
Will be granted and awarded by the goddess that I ask.
I will soon be progressing with your divine blessing."

After you've recited the spell, close it by adding *"So mote it be."* Keep the Brigid doll in your home throughout the course of spring to bring you good luck and blessings in the months ahead.

OSTARA

(VERNAL EQUINOX) | MARCH 20—23

At this time of year, the warmth begins to wax and light overshadows the darkness—the spring equinox is approaching. Although Easter was adopted as a Christian festival, the word *Easter* derives from the

Germanic goddess Éostre, goddess of the dawn, spring, and fertility. This pagan Sabbat (also called Eostre or Eastre) was a fertile time, symbolizing the birth of all things new. Villagers celebrated by planting crops. Witches made a special effort to improve their lives so they could relish the remainder of the year without encountering any complications. Spells were cast to shake off bad luck, leaving a positive and motivated frame of mind. Today, many European witches use this time to rejoice in the wellbeing of women and fertility. We use this time to call upon her to help us become more independent, self-sufficient, and successful in the coming year.

Ostara Elements and Traditions

- **CANDLES** Ostara favors candles that are made from pale green, purple, and yellow. Traditionally, these candles are burned on the spring equinox.

  - **CRYSTALS** Amazonite, azurite, citrine, lapis lazuli

  - **DEITIES** Freya (Norse), Ostara (Germanic), Osiris (Egyptian)

- **HARE** Represents fertility and rebirth; more commonly known as the Easter bunny but is in fact a lunar animal sacred to Ostara

- **HERBS** Lavender, lilac, lovage, marjoram, tarragon, thyme

- **EGGS** Offer a promise of new life; thought to be an image of the universe; hold a balance of masculine and feminine, with the yolk, representing the sun god, enclosed within the white, or the goddess. Eggs were often blown and decorated to give as gifts. Alternatively, once the egg was dry from blowing, one would write wishes on the shell and then plant it in the ground. Alternatively, bury an egg in a pot and leave it outside your home's entrance to attract wealth and abundance.

- **FLOWERS** Daffodils, crocus, violets, and pussy willow; flowers are brought into the home to bring light and blessings.

- **OSTARA BUNS** Baking is a given during any of the Wiccan Sabbats, so Ostara is a time to make and bake Ostara buns, or hot cross buns. The perimeter of the bun represents the wheel of the year, and the cross in the center is the Celtic cross.

- **TREES** Ash, alder, and birch; leaves and twigs from trees are decorated with spring-colored ribbons and placed on the altar during rituals.

An Ostara Spell for Removing Obstacles

Ostara is a perfect backdrop for rituals that change one's luck from bad to good, for healing and health, and for removing blocks and obstacles. If you or someone you know is at a standstill in life and seems to be blocked from every angle, or even if you simply want to safeguard yourself against obstacles, this spell will thwart any negative energy, giving you and your aura a thorough spring-clean.

Materials

A single spring flower, such as daffodil, crocus, or violet

Candles, in pale green, purple, or yellow

Hot cross buns, homemade or store-bought

A medium bowl

Bark or twigs, from ash, alder, or birch

Hare ornament, to represent Ostara (optional)

An amazonite stone

Ritual

On the spring equinox, set up your altar and place a single spring flower in the center. Choose a candle and light it next to the flower. Make or buy some hot cross buns, place a few in the bowl, and set the bowl next to the candle. To the altar add some bark, twigs, or even a hare ornament. While the candle burns, empower a piece of amazonite (see chapter 2, pages 29–35) with intent. Visualize yourself running through a spring meadow, as free as a bird, stopping every now and again to smell the flowers. This is a time when you can let your imagination run away and create your own little fantasy. After a few minutes of this, rest the stone directly in front of the candle and say the following incantation three times:

"This Ostara I cleanse my space, removing blocks from every place,
Peace in my heart and calmness of mind, an easy path ahead I'll find."

After you've recited the spell three times, close it by adding *"So mote it be."*
While the candle is burning, take the amazonite in one hand and eat one of the
hot cross buns with the other. Allow the candle to burn down. You might want
to give the remaining buns to family members so that they can also receive the
magickal blessing.

When the candle has burned down, press the flower in a heavy book for a week
or so. Save this flower for any other spells you might want to cast during the spring
months. The stone should be kept in the home for the foreseeable future. Don't
throw away any other altar items; just keep them in a safe place to use later.

An Ostara Spell to Celebrate Womanhood

Although men do practice Wicca, there seem to be
more women with a fascination for the craft. If you
want to rejoice in being a woman, this simple Ostara
spell will engulf you in good fortune and help
you flourish.

Materials

> A small citrine crystal
>
> A tealight oil burner
>
> Jasmine oil
>
> Water
>
> Bark, from birch (optional)
>
> A tealight candle, in white

You can cast this spell at any time during the first week of the spring equinox, and you don't necessarily need to set up an altar, either. Cleanse and empower your crystal (see chapter 2, pages 29–35) before resting it in the dish of the oil burner. Add a few drops of jasmine oil to the crystal in the dish and then top it up with water. If you can get birch bark, break a little bit off and place it in the water with the crystal. If you don't manage to locate any, then don't worry; the spell will still work. Light the candle underneath the oil burner and let the smell from the oil permeate the room for about an hour. Make sure you stay in the room during this time to receive the blessing. Say the following spell seven times:

"In the year to come I will strive to be the very best that I can be,
Like the clearest star I'll glow and shine, and joyful success will all be mine."

After you've recited the spell seven times, close the ritual by adding *"So mote it be."* You can now go about your business, but the candle must be allowed to burn down, so be prepared to top up the water in the dish if it evaporates. Once the candle has extinguished itself, leave the crystal to cool and then remove and dry it. This crystal is now super magickal, so keep it with you to use as a lucky talisman.

BELTANE

APRIL 30—MAY 1

Beltane translates as "the bright fire" and is usually celebrated from April 30 to May 1 (May Day) or halfway between the spring equinox and the summer solstice. This is a historical Gaelic fire festival, traditionally commemorated by lighting bonfires, then driving cattle around the fires to bless them in the months ahead. Any hearth fires would be extinguished at Beltane and a new one lit. Today, Beltane is a favorite Sabbat among witches. It marks the beginning of summer and is a time to rejoice in warmer weather, a fruitful growing season, and, hopefully, happy times to come.

Sexuality, love, and fertility are also emphasized parts of Beltane. These days sex in rituals is not commonplace, but if you decide to make an exception, Beltane is the right time to do so. When it comes to conception, it is believed that making love outside, under the stars (and in a private place), will ripen your chances of fertility. Conduct your Beltane ritual outdoors by lighting a fire, then making love on the ground.

Beltane Elements and Traditions

- **BASKETS** These encourage lots of successful accomplishments when given as gifts; should be wicker, but shape doesn't matter; place apple blossoms and flowers inside before tying the handles with ribbons

- **CANDLES** Red, green, white, silver

- **CROWNS** In many of our ancient Beltane rituals it was the custom for the women of the villages to wear homemade crowns, crafted from wire and decorated with attached flowers. Many witches today like to make a crown so that they can wear it during their Beltane rituals, too.

- **CRYSTALS** Carnelian, garnet, malachite, moss agate, tiger's eye

- **DEITIES** Belenus, Green Man (Pagan/Celtic); Flora (Roman)

- **FAERIES** The veil that separates the earth plane from the faerie realm is said to lift around the time of Beltane. Faeries have always been held in high regard by witches and are honored with food offerings.

- **FIRE** Bonfires are traditionally lit on May Day to help cleanse the land and its occupants of any disease. Today, witches still perform fire rituals by gathering with likeminded people, lighting a bonfire, and dancing around it.

- **FLOWERS** Bluebells, roses, marigolds, and pansy flowers are just some of the plants that represent this time of year. Beltane is all about love, and flowers are picked and given to sweethearts as a gesture of devotion. Adorn your altar with any wild-growing flowers you can find.

- **HERBS** Mugwort, rosemary, lilac, angelica, frankincense

- **INCENSE** Jasmine, musk, rose, vanilla

- **MAYPOLE** The maypole was part of European folk pageants, and on May Day people attached ribbons and cords to a tree and danced around it. It's not the easiest of tasks to create a full-size maypole in the garden, but if you wanted to have a bash, it would be a great centerpiece for a Beltane party. Nowadays witches like to make miniature maypoles to place on the altar. They do this by sourcing a dowel rod about 2 feet (60 cm) in length, securing it to a wooden circular base, and gluing or attaching ribbons to the top.

- **RAINWATER** Witches treasure rainwater and can sometimes be seen collecting it. Europe tends to be showery in May, and with the promise of better things to come, the rain caught and collected at this time will serve well in any ritual. The water is used for bathing candles or dabbing on the witch's wrist before a spell commences.

- **RIBBONS** Beautify your altar with ribbons colored red, yellow, purple, blue, green, and white.

- **TREES** Hawthorn, ash, oak

A Beltane Spell

Fertility, happiness, concentration and achievements are good focuses for rituals performed during Beltane. Any of the fertility spells listed in chapter 5 on pages 126–28 work well, but a "kinfolk spell" can bring happiness and laughter to the home and all who reside there.

Materials

- A piece of crystal (see "Beltane Elements and Traditions")
- As many pieces of paper as there are people in your family and a pencil
- Three 3-foot (1-m) ribbons, in purple, white, and green
- Two candles, in white
- A feast of spring foods

Ritual

Cleanse and empower your crystal (see chapter 2, pages 29–35). On as many pieces of paper as there are people in your family, write the following incantation:

"We celebrate this Beltane with food and with flame;
we give you our thanks for uniting us again.
Happiness and joy reign in this house, all who dwell are blessed with this spell."

Faerie Chair

To attract fae folk into your garden, create a faerie ring of stones on the ground and situate a small white chair in the center. Plant some ivy at the base and scatter some climbing plant seeds in the ground so that, when they sprout, they will entwine around the chair. On May 1, tie some silver ribbons to the back of the chair, then sit and wait. If you are lucky enough, you might see some dancing lights or even spot a faerie out of the corner of your eye.

Knot together all three ribbons at the top and braid them, wrapping one ribbon over the other. Each member of the family must take a turn in crossing over the ribbon until all of it is braided. Tie a knot to secure it. Place this braid in a long length down the center of a table and light both candles, placing one at each end. Cook and prepare a feast of spring foods, such as salads, breads, cabbage, some nice cooked meats, and, for dessert, rhubarb crumble and cream or perhaps some fresh fruits. Lay the feast on the table. When everyone is seated, give each person a copy of the written incantation. Pass the empowered crystal from person to person before finally placing it somewhere on top of the braided ribbon. Together, read the incantation three times.

When you have all recited the spell, the person at the head of the table must close the ritual by saying, *"So mote it be."* Then proceed to enjoy your meal.

After the feast, clear everything away, but leave the crystal at the center of the table for a few months. Make sure you gather together regularly to eat your meals, and the magick will continue to flow.

LITHA

(SUMMER SOLSTICE) | JUNE 19–25

We have at last reached one of the most poignant moments in the Wiccan calendar—Litha, or the summer solstice. Midsummer, approximately June 19–25, brings us the longest days and shortest nights (though the dates do vary with geography and culture). Everything in the world is blooming with fruitfulness, the goddess is heavily pregnant with child, and the sun god is at his peak of virility. At this time, witches and druids celebrate the dawn and often stay up to watch the sunrise. This is a fertile time when we can rejoice in the abundance of life; however, despite this climax, we are also aware that darkness is ahead. From here on, as the sun begins to wane, the days will become shorter and the nights longer, and soon the cycle of life will be complete.

Litha Elements and Traditions

- **ACORNS** A symbol for fertility and prosperity, acorns are widely used as a talismans during Mabon and Midsummer. They are carried to ensure a long and rich life and sometimes are placed on windowsills during storms to ward off lightning.

- **BONFIRE** On Midsummer's Eve, people stay up all through the night to welcome the sunrise. Bonfires made from oak are lit on top of hills and mountains to pay respect to the sun. Once the coals die, they can be scattered atop crops, ensuring a good harvest. To re-create this on a small scale, you could light a small bonfire in your garden and spread the cooled coals over your plants.

- **CANDLES** Blue, yellow, orange, green; anoint with lavender oil

- **COLORS** There is an abundance of colors to work with: green for the grass, blue for the skies, and orange for the sun. Yellows, pinks, purples, and reds represent blooms. Take your pick!

- **CRYSTALS** Amber, tiger's eye, jade, onyx

- **DEITIES** Apollo, Hestia (Greek); Aten (Egyptian)

- **ELDERFLOWER** This plant is sacred to the mother goddess and is often referred to as the witches' tree. It gives magickal healing vibes and so is picked to make wines, tonics, and juices.

- **FAERIES** Midsummer is a time when faerie folk come out to play. Hang pretty, sparkly objects from the branches of trees to attract them.

- **FLOWERS** Carnations, daisies, honeysuckle, sunflowers, and roses.

- **HERBS** Basil, chamomile, fennel, lavender, lemon balm, mugwort, thyme, St. John's wort, sandalwood, saffron, and vervain

  - **HONEY** The full moon at Midsummer is sometimes called a "honey moon"—a time around the summer solstice when handfastings and marriages are common. Witches like to drink warm honey to celebrate the sun god, believing it has life-giving properties. Honey cakes are also baked and blessed throughout the cooking process, then placed on the altar during midsummer ceremonies to bring health and healing to all who eat it.

  - **INCENSE** Lemon, rose, wisteria

- **TREES** Bay, beech, oak; the mighty strength of the oak tree has always held a great deal of significance at Midsummer. Offerings from the oak tree were brought into the house to adorn the altar, giving rituals more potency.

A Litha Spell

The power from the sun during midsummer means any spells can be cast at this time, but focus on happiness, movement, and change. The force from the sun's rays will only enhance your magick and bring successful results. Honor the sun and ask it to bless you with abundance and happiness.

Materials

A glass bowl

Enough tap or rainwater to fill the bowl halfway

A piece of crystal (see list on page 279)

A floating candle, to represent the sun

Ritual

It's best to perform this ritual on a day with fair weather. Half fill the bowl with water (tap water is fine, but rainwater is better). Cleanse and empower your crystal (see chapter 2, pages 29–35), telling it exactly how you would like to be blessed, before placing it in the water. Rest the floating candle on top of the crystal. Bring the bowl outside into your garden or a different outdoor spot, like a quiet park or safe wooded area. Place the bowl on the ground, light the candle, and chant the following spell seven times:

> *"Sun god, cast down your blessings on nature, land, and seas,*
> *Your rays will shine down bright; fill my bowl with light."*

After you've recited the spell seven times, close the ritual by adding *"So mote it be."* Take some time to stay outdoors and sit quietly with Mother Nature. After about thirty minutes, blow out the candle, collect the bowl, and head back indoors. Place the bowl on your altar and relight the candle. Allow it to burn down.

When your candle extinguishes itself, your crystal will be super empowered. Keep it close by through the coming weeks in order to better receive your blessings. This ritual can be repeated for any Sabbat, not just Litha. Tap into the power with a crystal for each celebration.

LAMMAS

JULY 31 (SUNSET)—AUGUST 1

Lammas (also called Lughnasadh or "loaf mass," or Pagan Thanksgiving) commemorates the first grain harvest of the year. This is an ancient, celebratory event when the earth's growth slows and the sun and moon—aka the god and goddess—are bound together, providing plentiful crops to store throughout the winter months ahead. The garden is all-important to modern witches, so Wiccan growers often take this opportunity to stockpile their food, blanching homegrown vegetables to freeze and eat at a later date. Witches often freeze or dry their herbs for use in spells and recipes during the colder months. The making of jam and chutney is also traditional at Lammas, so roll up your sleeves and get to work in the kitchen. This time is also about embracing creativity and harvesting not just food but also memories of your own personal achievements.

Lammas Elements and Traditions

- **CANDLES** The sun is at its warmest and is high in the sky, so choose candle colors such as oranges and yellows.

- **COLORS** Anything representing fall; green, brown, yellow, orange

- **CORN POPPET** Little poppets and ornamental charms made from corn are placed on the altar in thanks to Mother Earth for her many offerings. They are a symbol of good luck and fertility. If you are a creative sort, you can make your own, but if not, they can be purchased cheaply.

- **CRYSTALS** Agate, carnelian, citrine, jasper, peridot, moonstone

- **DEITIES** Áine, Cerridwen, and Lugh (Celtic); Demeter (Greek)

- **FLOWERS** Sunflowers are by far the most general to use in spellcraft at this time of year because their heads are heavy with seed. Witches sometimes make sunflower crowns to wear during rituals. The calendula flower is also a popular choice; its dried petals are used in spells for thankfulness and healing.

- **HERBS** All grains, such as oats, barley, and rye; meadowsweet is a preferred choice for anything relating to love and marriage. Mint is usually present on a Lammas altar, as it offers protection and healing and draws in prosperity.

- **TREES** Beech, hawthorn, sycamore

- **INCENSE** Rose, sandalwood

- **ONION GARLANDS** Onions not only taste good; they soak up negativity in the home, so braids and garlands can be hung in windows to ward off sickness and evil. Garlic garlands can be used in the same way.

A Lammas Spell and Recipe for Wish Powder

Spellwork during Lammas can remove negativity, curses, and bad luck and provide protection. Spells during this time should also focus on gratitude, guide communication, invoking angels, and one's desires and wishes.

Lammas is a time when you can ask the universe for anything you might need to make life more comfortable. Wish Powder in particular works well for almost anything you desire (if the need is genuine and you are not doing it for any kind of greedy, personal gain).

Materials

A small container with a snap-on lid

A piece of crystal
(see "Lammas Elements and Traditions")

3 teaspoons of dried meadowsweet

A handful of calendula petals

3 teaspoons of dried basil

3 teaspoons of dried mint

A small pot of biodegradable glitter, in silver, to represent your wishes

Items that represent Lammas (see "Lammas Elements and Traditions" for inspiration)

A tall tapered candle, in yellow or orange

Ritual

To make Wish Powder, you will need a small plastic container with a snap-on lid. Cleanse and empower your crystal (see chapter 2, pages 29–35). Add to the container the dried meadowsweet, calendula petals, dried basil, and dried mint. Put the crystal into the container with your herbs and petals. Empty a small pot of silver biodegradable glitter into the container. Stir everything together with your hand. Seal the container.

On the evening of August 1, set up your altar, placing any items that represent Lammas on its surface. Light the candle. Hold it in one hand and the container in the other. Say the following spell seven times:

"Enchanted powder inside this dish,
be ever powerful, grant my wish."

After you've recited the spell seven times, close the ritual by adding *"So mote it be."* Place the container and candle on your altar, and allow the flame to burn for a couple of hours before blowing it out. After the candle has been allowed to burn, bring your container of Wish Powder outside. Take a pinch of the powder and throw it into the night sky while silently making a wish. In the coming months, or when you feel that you need something, relight the candle next to the powder and repeat the incantation.

As a general note, do be realistic with your wishes. The universe may have made it possible for us to plant corn, but it definitely draws the line at planting sawdust! Keep this in mind, and your wishes should come to fruition.

MABON

(AUTUMNAL EQUINOX) | SEPTEMBER 20—23

Traditionally, this festival was all about giving thanks to the Welsh god Mabon. He is said to be the child of the Earth Mother and the god Modron, although the deities vary with every culture. For example, the druids paid tribute to the Green Man and gave food offerings to trees to mark their respect, whereas the Pagans honored the mature goddess as she passed from mother to crone. Now, as the year begins to wane, quietly reflect and look back over the past months. This is the second harvest, the autumn equinox, a thoughtful time when our ancestors accumulated the harvest they had labored so hard to produce.

In modern Wicca, we see Mabon as a period of contemplation, but we also use it as a time to clear out any clutter and recycle things we no longer need. The expression "Tidy house, tidy mind" is the focus here. Creating order surrounded by neatness and harmony in life brings a sense of pleasure and contentment.

Elements and Traditions

• **APPLES** Although we traditionally associate this fruit with Samhain, Mabon is a perfect time to celebrate the humble apple. When you cut an apple in half widthwise, you will see the sign of a pentagram. If you cut it in half down its length, the symbol inside is of the female genitalia. Because of their magickal significance, apples are often present on the altar during Mabon festivals.

- **CANDLE COLORS** Red, green, orange, yellow, or any color representing fall

- **CRYSTALS** Amber, hematite, red aventurine, sunstone, yellow topaz, clear quartz, citrine, peridot, lapis lazuli

- **DEITIES** Green Man, Triple Goddess (Pagan); Modron (Welsh); Persephone (Greek); Pomona (Roman); Thor (Germanic/Norse)

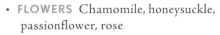

- **FLOWERS** Chamomile, honeysuckle, passionflower, rose

- **FRUITS** Pomegranate, berries, apples, pears, plums

- **HERBS** Ferns, ivy, milkweed, myrrh, sage, saffron, thistle, tobacco, yarrow

- **HORN OF PLENTY** Baskets made in the shape of horns are filled with fruits and embellished with flowers to represent all things in abundance. Modern witches often wear cornucopia jewelry to symbolize luck. Meditate on the horn of life, which showers money and blessings.

- **INCENSE** Benzoin, frankincense, myrrh, sage

- **TREES** Gratitude trees are made at Mabon to give thanks to Mother Earth for her endless abundance; acorn, walnut, pine

A Mabon Spell

Mabon is a great time for prosperity and money rituals, and for spells concerning security, safety, protection, and confidence. This is definitely the best time of year to cast spells for financial security, so perform a general money spell, like the one given here, on September 21. For the best results, use two small pieces of sunstone.

Materials

Two small pieces of sunstone

An apple, any kind

A paring knife

Two tealight candles, in red, green, orange, or yellow

Items that represent Mabon (see lists on pages 286–87 for inspiration)

Ritual

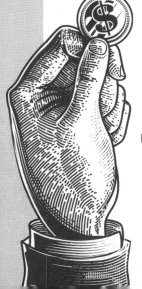

Cleanse and empower your crystals (see chapter 2, pages 29–35). The empowering process should be performed for at least thirty minutes or for as long as possible. Hold a piece of sunstone in each hand and sit quietly, imagining that an upturned, pure-gold cornucopia is spilling gold coins all over your body. Silently ask the universe to bless you with a better financial situation and envisage yourself paying off all your bills and debts with ease.

Place the crystals on the altar and prepare your apple by cutting it in half, widthwise, with the knife. Notice that the seeded area in each half forms a pentacle star. Your apple is going to act as a receptacle for your candles, so you might need to slice the bottom of each apple half so it sits flat on a surface. Carefully cut in a circle around the stars, carving out a hole in each apple half. You will need to make this hole large enough to place a tealight candle in each piece. Place the apples side by side on your altar and drop a tealight candle inside of each one before lighting them. Finally, place the crystals directly in front of each of the apples.

You can now decorate your altar with anything representing Mabon. Food offerings like bread and fruits, flowers, herbs, and plants create the perfect ambience. Some witches like to gather a selection of different twigs from the garden and place them in a vase, tying each twig with ribbons in autumnal shades. These can be as simple or as decorative as you like. When you are finished, recite the following spell seven times:

> *"I call upon the god and goddess to bring stability to*
> *my life and grace me with a purse of wealth,*
> *I show gratitude and thankfulness for your blessings already bestowed.*
> *Turn around my fortune and let me sleep easy, knowing*
> *that my financial life is settled and in balance."*

After you've recited the spell seven times, close the ritual by adding *"So mote it be."* When you have completed the incantation, allow the candles to burn down until they extinguish themselves. Take both halves of the apple and place them as an offering under a tree. The crystals must be kept somewhere in the home. In the coming weeks, your finances may start to look more promising.

SAMHAIN

(ALL HALLOW'S EVE) | OCTOBER 31

Samhain, or Sow Wen, is an ancient Gaelic festival recognized as one of the most prominent events in a witch's calendar. It is considered by some to be the most important holiday of all. During Samhain, the Sun King is surrendered to the earth, and the crone will grieve him until he is reborn again at Yule. Samhain, which is sometimes referred to as All Hallow's Eve, the Feast of the Dead, All Souls' Night, or Halloween, marks the final chapter of birth and death and makes way for the last harvest of the year. The seeds from crops and plants fall back into the ground and lie lifeless until the cycle once again begins.

From a magickal point of view, this is a time when the veil separating the spirit world from the earth is lifted, meaning we can communicate with the dead and lost loved ones. Centuries ago, people would dress up in scary costumes to frighten away evil spirits that might walk through the veil. For witches today, All Hallow's Eve is even more important than Yule, as it is considered to be our new year. It is an incredibly powerful time when magick amplifies, divination intensifies, and spells and rituals become more potent. A favorite tradition is to cast a spell for each family member. Write down their need on paper and light them a candle during the evening of Samhain. Then say the following words for every member:

"Powers climb into the night, with this candle that I light,

Wishes granted with what I write, magick comes with joyful light. So mote it be."

There is also no better time than Samhain to have a party, but a witch's gathering is not of the usual ghostly, ghoulish variety. Invite friends and family to feast on pumpkin soup, breads, seasonal meats, and vegetables. Cast spells for the good of mankind (and drink a little too much homemade wine).

Elements and Traditions

- **APPLES** Apples represent immortality. Our ancestors buried apples on All Hallow's Eve as food offerings to the souls waiting to be reborn. Bobbing for apples had a more romantic connotation and was thought to predict the future. In one variation of the game, apples were placed in a barrel, and each one would represent a young woman's potential suitor. The maiden would then bob for an apple, and if she managed to bite into it and lift it on the first attempt, she was destined for romance. In another game, a group of women would race to the barrel and the first to retrieve an apple would be first to marry.

- **BROOMSTICK** Besoms, or broomsticks, were made from the twigs of birch. They were used in rituals to sweep away energies from the past months, leaving auras spick-and-span for the new year.

- **CANDLES AND COLORS** All autumnal shades, like orange, red, green, gold, and yellow

  - **CRYSTALS** Black obsidian, calcite, carnelian, danburite, opal, spirit quartz, sunstone

  - **DEITIES** Anubis, Osiris (Egyptian); Cerridwen (Celtic); Horned God (Pagan); Hecate, Persephone (Greek); Hel, Odin (Germanic/Norse); Oya (Yoruba)

  - **INCENSE** Sandalwood and sweetgrass

- **FLOWERS AND PLANTS** All fall flowers, vervain, apples, oak leaves

- **HERBS** Bay, rosemary, mugwort

- **PUMPKIN** Gourds were carved into jack-o'-lanterns and placed on doorsteps to welcome deceased relatives.

- **TREES** Rowan, birch

A Samhain Spell

A nice traditional exercise to do at Samhain is to reach out and communicate with any deceased loved ones. Perform this ritual during the evening of October 31.

Materials

A piece of spirit quartz

A sprig of fresh rosemary

A small dish

1 teaspoon of dried vervain

½ teaspoon of white pepper

1 bay leaf

A photograph of your deceased loved one(s)

A candle, in purple

Ritual

Cleanse your crystal (see chapter 2, pages 29–35). To empower the crystal, cup it in your hands and think about your loved one and gather your memories of time you spent together. After doing this for a few minutes, place the crystal on the altar, then tear the leaves the rosemary sprig and place them in the dish. Add to the dish the dried vervain, white pepper, and bay leaf. Rest a photograph of your deceased loved one on the altar and place the crystal on top. Light a purple candle and say the following incantation thirteen times:

> *"I raise the veil and call out to you; see my face, hear my voice,*
> *This Samhain I summon you and speak with you; this is my choice,*
> *I raise the veil and reach to you; feel my touch, sense my power."*

After you've recited the spell thirteen times, close the ritual by adding *"So mote it be."* While the candle is burning, talk aloud to your loved one. You can say anything you want; this is your time to express your feelings and be at one with them. It is not uncommon for you to sense that you are not alone. When the candle has burned for about an hour, extinguish it; then take the bowl of herbs and the crystal and place them next to your bed. If your loved one has heard your message, they may visit you in your dreams.

A SPECIAL MESSAGE FROM
LEANNA AND SHAWN

Years ago, when we were young witches, Wicca, or any faith coupled with the craft, still had an element of shame attached to it. You had to be pretty daring to admit to anyone that you had an interest in witchcraft, not to mention that you cast spells for a pastime! Over the years, we have known people who crossed the street so they would not to have to talk to us. On one occasion a priest even told me (Leanna) that he would pray for my soul. Of course, this attitude stems from a lack of knowledge; those who mock Wiccans do not fully understand the gentle nature and purity of witchcraft. For Wicca practitioners, it is not a religion and it is not a cult—it is a way of life born from the oldest faith in the world, and it's a personal belief system that we can mold in any way we want.

Over the past twenty years or so, something wonderful has happened: thousands of witches are stepping out of the broom closet. Thanks to the connection granted by social media and a better understanding of history, we can now stand proud and admit to all and sundry that we practice magick. The stigma is leaving, and the honor is restored. The younger generation is embracing the craft, and the more mature are finally peeking into their own spirituality. We have come full circle, from the ancient ancestors who believed wholeheartedly in the gods and goddesses, to the present day, where those same deities are being revered once again.

If you decide to carry crystals close to your heart while embarking on your Wiccan journey, be aware it may take you many years to learn all about their individual, magickal uses. For us, magickal stones have become a very significant part of our craft, used regularly in our rituals and in our everyday lives. Remember, you are an individual, so you must listen to your own truth and journey, going along this path at your own pace. This path is no one else's story; it is yours!

Acknowledgments

At sterling, vision becomes wisdom, and we would like to thank our brilliant editor, Barbara Berger, for her foresight in turning *The Crystal Witch* into a sparkling gem with her magickal editorial skills.

And, to our agent, Bill Gladstone, at Waterside Productions, knowing is believing, and we thank you for believing in us.

Also at Sterling, we are also grateful to cover art director Elizabeth Lindy for the beautiful cover design; Sharon Jacobs for the stunning interior design conception, direction, and layout; production editor Ellina Litmanovich; and production manager Terence Campo. We also thank editor Kayla Overbey for her discerning eye.

PICTURE CREDITS

INDEX

Beryllonite, **62**, 93, 96

Birthstones, 233

Bixbite, **62**, 94, 96

Black, intentions/themes, 6

Bloodstone (heliotrope), **45**, 52, **63**, 93, 94, 96, 135, 197, 233, 245

Blue, intentions/themes, 6

Boji stone, **63**

Bowenite, **63**, (94–96)

Brazilianite, **63**, 92

Brigid (goddess), 267, 268

Bronzite, **63**, 93

Brookite, **63**, 96

Brown, intentions/themes, 6

Bullying, guarding against, *104–5*

Bustamite, **63**, 91, 93

C

Cacoxenite, **63**, 93. *See also* Amethyst-cacoxenite

Calcite, **63–64**, (91–96), 106, 154–55, 197, 203, 239, 242, 243, 292

Candles
  about: bringing crystal facets to life, 37
  anointing, 38–39
  colors and their intentions/themes, 6–7
  preparing for crystal ritual, 37–39, 98–99
  types for altar, 8

Career. *See* Employment/work

Caring for crystals, overview of, 27

Carnelian, **46**, 52, 58, **64**, (92–95)
  seasonal celebration uses, 275, 283, 292
  zodiac associations, 234, 235, 239, 241

Cassiterite, **64**, 91, 92

Catlinite, **64**, 96

Cavansite, **64**, 92

Celebrations. *See* Annual festivities

Celestite (celestine), **46**, 52, **64**, 93, 96, 261

Chakras
  balancing, crystals and, 15
  blocked, clearing, 56
  Crown with, 56
  Heart, 39, 55, 69, 87, 155
  Root, 55
  Sacral, 55, 74
  Solar Plexus, 55, 73
  Third Eye, 22, 36, 84, 181, 192, 197, 198, 254
  Throat, 55, 59, 88

Chalcanthite, **65**, 91, 94

Chalcedony, **65**, (91–93), 109–10, 236, 237, 242, 243. *See also* Carnelian; Onyx

Chalcopyrite, **65**, 92, 95

Charging (empowering) crystals, 33–35, 97, 98, 99, 194–95

Charoite, **65**, 92

Children, having. *See* Fertility/birth

Children, spells to help, 100–107. *See also* Emotions/well-being
  guarding against bullying, *104–5*
  helping child sleep at night, *102–3*
  helping concentration, *106*
  increasing patience and, *107*
  protecting a child, *101–2*

Choosing crystals, 18–23

Chrysoberyl, **65**, 92, 94, 95, 199

Chrysocolla, **65**, 94, 125

Chrysoprase, **65**, 92, 93, 95

Circle (crystal), creating, 131–32

Circular grids, 224–25

Citrine, **47**, 52, **65**, 91, 94, 95, (252–54), 264. *See also* Ametrine
  birthstone, 233
  pendulum with, 203
  seasonal celebration uses, 271, 283, 287
  spells using, 157–58, 273–74
  zodiac associations, 234, 238

Cleansing crystals, 29–32

Clinochlore, **65**. *See also* Seraphinite

Closing ritual, 99

Cloth, altar, 8

Colors, intentions/themes, 6–7

Communication, 91, *168*

Concentration, helping, *106*

Confidence, 91

Connecting with crystals, 19–21

Cookeite, **65**

Corundum. *See* Rubies; Sapphires

Covellite (Covelline), **66**, 92

Creativity, crystals for, 91

Creedite, **66**, 94

Crowns, crystal, 223–24

Crystallomancy (crystal ball gazing), 198–202. *See also* Scrying

Crystals. *See also* specific crystals
  about: overview of Wicca and, 1–3
  charging/empowering, 33–35, 97, 98, 99, 194–95
  choosing, 18–23
  cleansing, 29–32
  communication of/with, 17
  finding, picking up, 25
  as gifts, 25
  incorporating into spellcasting, 10
  listening for yours, 21–23
  magic with, how it works, 16–17

Sunstone, **87**, 145, 158–59, 287, 288–89, 292

Surgery, spell for after, *136*

T

Taaffeite, **87**

Talking to pendulums, 205–6

Tanzanite, **87**, 94, 233

Tarot readings, crystal, 206–9

Tea, crystal, for divination, 209–10

Tektite, **87**, 92, 95. *See also* Moldavite

Third eye (and Third Eye Chakra), 22, 36, 84, 181, 192, 197, 198, 254

Thulite, **87**, 91

Tibetan bells, 32

Tiffany stone (purple passion), **87**, 92, 94

Tiger iron (mugglestone), **88**

Tiger's eye, **50**, 52, **88**, 91, (94–96), 101–2, 122–23, 238, 275, 279

Toolkit. *See also* Candles; *specific crystals*
    about: overview of, 36
    essential crystals, 40–52
    wands, 53–56

Topaz, **88**, 91, 92, 95, 96
    birthstone, 233
    seasonal celebration uses, 264, 287
    zodiac associations, 235, 238, 239, 241, 242, 244

"Topping up" your stone, 99

Touch, Reiki and, 246–54

Tourmaline, **51**, 52, **88**, (92–96), 230, 251, 264
    about: types, colors, and effects, **88**
    birthstone, 233
    crystal crown with, 224
    rubellite, 83
    spells using, 119, 140–41, 166–67
    zodiac associations, 236, 237, (240–43)

Travel, protection for. *See* Protection

Tremolite, **89**, 93

Triphane, **86**, 93

Tsavorite, **89**, 95

Tugtupite, **89**, 94

Turquoise, **51**, 52, 75, **89**, 95, 175–76, 198, 252, 254
    birthstone, 233
    zodiac associations, 236, 242, 243, 245

U

Ulexite, **89**, 92

Unakite, **89**

Unakite jasper, **73**, 94, 95

V

Vanadinite, **89**, 91, 94

Variscite, **89**, 92

Verdite, **89**, 96

Vesuvianite, **89**, 92

Vitalite, **89**

Vivianite, **89**, 93

Vortexite, **89**, 96

W

Wands, 53–56

Water, items that represent, 9

Wavellite, **90**, 92

Wearing crystals, 1, 15, 230, 254, 261

Welcoming new crystal, 23–24

Well-being. *See* Emotions/well-being

White, intentions/themes, 7

Wiccan Rede (rules), 11

Wicca, overview of crystals and, 1–3

Wildlife, protecting/connecting with, *161–62*

Willemite, **90**, 95

Wish powder recipe, Lammas spell and, *284–85*

Womanhood, Ostara spell to celebrate, *273–74*

Work. *See* Employment/work; Money

Wulfenite, **90**, 94

Y

Yellow, intentions/themes, 7

Yule (winter solstice), 263–66

Z

Zebra stone, **90**, 93

Zincite, **90**, 93, 94

Zircon, **90**, 93, 95, 233

Zodiac, crystals for, 232–45

Zoisite, **90**, 92, 93